The

Complete
Teacher

The

Complete
Teacher

Thought-Provoking Ideas for
Balanced and Meaningful Teaching

Greg Noyes

The Complete Teacher

Thought-Provoking Ideas for Balanced and Meaningful Teaching

Greg Noyes

ISBN (Print Edition): 978-1-09832-729-3

ISBN (eBook Edition): 978-1-09832-730-9

To

Natalie, my wife, my navigator, and my inspiration.

Matt, Abbie, Belle, and Max, my world and legacy.

Mom and Dad, a wealth of wisdom and support.

Contents

Acknowledgements

This book has been many years in the making and it would not have been possible without God's grace and the community that he placed around me.

I want to thank my master teacher Ken and the rest of the Roadrunner crew for taking me in. Chris, thank you for always allowing me to watch you teach and inspire students. These formative years working at James Rutter Middle School opened up my mind to just how amazing teaching could be. Richard, Mike, and Yuri, you showed me ways that I could lead at school and afforded me so many opportunities to do just that. I truly found a diamond in the rough with you all in this amazing community.

I am deeply grateful to Bob and Anne, who believed in me and took the time to mentor me. Bob, I could always rely on you for sound advice and for having anecdotes to match any situation we faced. Anne, your ability to navigate situations, connect with staff, and operate with efficiency greatly impacted how I lead. Cory, Dena, Peatra, Steven, Joel, Jamie, and Shavon, you are the team I grew with and was inspired by every day. Who knew that working together could be so much fun?

I could not have more appreciation for my mom and dad, who have supported me in every way imaginable. Mom, educator extraordinaire, you spent countless hours going over my ideas for this book and made sure I didn't leave out any thinkers, ideas or perspectives. You have always been my biggest fan. Dad, from all the years of little league coaching to helping me through college, you have always invested in me and had my back. Thank you for modeling what it means to work hard.

Grandma Nancy, I have you to thank for encouraging me to laugh more, to be playful, and to tell silly jokes. You are as witty as they come and have always brought joy to my life. Grandpa Paul, what a legacy you have impressed on me. Thank you for the Boo-Boo Bear stories and for loving me beyond words. I would be blessed to become half the man you are.

This acknowledgement would not be complete without boasting about the amazing friends I have in Justin, Bobby, Levi, Chris, and Nick. Through all seasons and challenges, you guys have always been there for me. From your jokes to your own professional journeys, I thought about each of you often while writing this book.

And finally, I want to thank my wife, Natalie. Truly, none of this would have happened without her. From reading early drafts, to organizing the publishing process, she made every aspect of this project better. She was as important to getting this book done as I was. She believed in my work, didn't allow me to settle, picked me up when I was down, engaged the kids when I needed to focus, and sat with me for hours on end to edit and dialogue. What an amazing partner I have in you, Natalie!

2 Corinthians 4:7

Preface

"Well, that pretty much covers it" was the phrase that stayed with me as I worked on this project. I set out to create, to summarize, to list and to categorize everything pertinent to the role of the teacher. But most of all, I wanted to help. I wanted to put together a book to help teachers, leaders of teachers, or anyone else engaged in the business of teaching and learning. In one sense, this book is more breadth than depth. Since the educational landscape is always changing, many of these topics will move in and out of the spotlight. I continue to learn new things every day, and I'm bound to overlook some educational topics, only touching upon subjects that deserve more careful examination.

I find inspiration in the bodies of work from educational masters like Stephen Covey on effectiveness, Robert Marzano on leadership, Michael Fullan on change, Carol Dweck on mindset, and Anthony Muhammad on culture. More recently, I have been drawn to Rick Wormeli and John Hattie on assessment, Carol Ann Tomlinson on differentiation, Zaretta Hammond and Christopher Emdin on cultural responsiveness. In addition to referencing the wisdom of top thinkers, I also draw from my own experiences and from the experiences of friends and colleagues throughout my career in education.

The concepts in this book are wide-ranging. Some are highly technical and research-based, while others are based on common sense and easily relatable. What the concepts share is the fact that they are applicable to any classroom teacher, practical for all grades, and purposeful for both rookie and veteran. Some topics will be pertinent to teachers in different ways. Just how pertinent will primarily depend on teacher mindset, and on grade level, subject area, school demographics, and school culture.

This book will address effective practices in the classroom; but it is far more than a book of strategies. Themes of this book also include leadership, classroom management, healthy life balance, and relationships with students. All 101 topics can be taken in turn, while together they paint a comprehensive picture for teachers in their profession, touching upon issues beyond the walls of the classroom such as the achievement gap, helicopter parents, and more. With emerging emphases on distance learning and virtual instruction, the thoughts and ideas in *The Complete Teacher* are as relevant as ever. These concepts will affirm what teachers already do well, challenge them to improve in new areas, and inspire them to search for more insight. In the end, *The Complete Teacher* to make teachers better. Both teachers and their students deserve that.

The Complete Teacher is written topically and the chapters can be read in any order. Read them in the order presented, or dive in where you would like. Either way, consider these seven recurring themes as you read.

- ASSESSMENT - anything related to measurement of learning. This includes concepts such as formative assessment, summative assessment, checking for understanding, gradual release, grading, homework, and more.

- BALANCE - universal thoughts on the teaching profession. Ideas involve balance within and without the workplace, managing stress, staying healthy, having fun, loving your job, and recognizing your career in an appropriate context.

- CONNECTIONS - building relationships with students. This incorporates notions such as building bridges with students and teaming with learners in ways that are empathetic, engaging, culturally responsive, and effective.

- LEADERSHIP - insight from both experts and novices on how to lead in the classroom, both formally and informally.

- MANAGEMENT - techniques for running a smooth classroom. These approaches touch upon the importance of accountability and routines, as well as proven ways to prevent poor behavior before it starts.

- PROFESSIONALISM - guidelines to conduct yourself in a manner that honors the teaching profession. Topics include communication, collaboration, how to be kind, and avoiding all things that may be deemed "unprofessional."

- TEACHING - best practices for teaching and learning. Ideas on how to excel when teaching and facilitating and how to encourage learning among students. These entries address effective techniques applied to the classroom.

It's More Than A Paycheck: Recognizing the Awesomeness That Is the Teacher

"If you can read this, thank a teacher." - American Proverb

There is a common teacher saying that goes something like, "We don't get into teaching for the money." This is a simple admission that a career in education, although it brings in a steady income, doesn't really compare to the income potential in other fields within the private sector. I distinctly remember my first paycheck as a full-time teacher. After years of school, teaching programs, student-teaching, and sporadic substitute work, it was a significant milestone for me. That initial paycheck was just over $2,600, which was slightly higher than the national average for teachers at that time. The best word to describe the paycheck was "plenty." Better yet, it was more than plenty.

I made my first major purchase with that paycheck, buying a $600 Taylor guitar. And after paying the rent and other bills, I still had plenty left over. Certainly, I'm not suggesting that teachers are overpaid or that they don't deserve to be fairly compensated. The point is that I was awestruck by the fact that I was getting paid to do something that I loved. I exulted in it to my family and friends. Being a teacher was the epitome of awesomeness.

That first year, I aimed to be both fun and challenging teaching history to middle school students. I loved my students and loved my content. In my own little corner of school, students came through my doors each day, and I was a celebrity. My calling and my purpose were finally coming to fruition. I recall asking myself, "Do I really get *paid* to do this?" The job was so incredible, so fulfilling, and so powerful, I didn't quite know what to do with it.

Eventually, that initial euphoria proved to be fleeting. Colleagues and administrators came and went. Each year brought new students, posed new challenges, and new growth areas were recognized. But throughout all the highs and lows, I remind myself (and others) that at the end of the day, we enjoy the privilege of teaching. What an amazing career we have chosen. As a teacher goes into year two, three, four, five, and beyond, it can be easy to lose sight of this first love. Students, curriculum, and school culture is always changing.

Look for new opportunities to fall in love with your work. And don't forget…we get paid to do it!

Action Steps:

> ➤ **Find an opportunity to tell your students why you decided to teach. They will listen.**

> ➤ **Find an opportunity to tell someone else why you decided to become a teacher. You never know who is waiting to be inspired.**

First Impressions: Focus on Yours, Forgive with Theirs

"You never get a second chance to make a first impression." - Will Rogers

"Almost everyone will make a good first impression, but only a few will make a good lasting impression." - Sonya Parker

Dr. Albert Mehrabian's groundbreaking 1967 communication study found that when a single word is spoken, judgment by the listener is 7% based on what is said, 38% based on how it was said, and 55% based on non-verbal communication from the speaker (Mehrabian, 1967). A more recent Princeton study suggests that first impressions are solidified in a tenth of a second (Todorov & Willis, 2006).

It's not impossible to overcome a poor first impression, but it can take time and effort. There is a great deal at stake in making first impressions. Although the 7%-38%-55% rule and the one-tenth of a second rule were results of very specific studies and are often misquoted, the concept of first impressions has enormous implications for educators, all of whom need to build positive relationships with new groups of students each year.

For teachers to make the most out of connections with students, first day impressions are vital. Students of all ages instantly pick up on attitude. Things like posture, smiles, eye contact, raised brows, handshakes, and forward leans have all been linked to positive first impressions. For example, do you stand at your door and greet students with a smile and handshake on the first day of school? Doing so will make the most of those crucial first encounters. What about your syllabus or parent letter? Is it overwhelming, hyper-focused on rules and consequences, or does it front-load and build excitement for learning? Beyond the first day of school, there are first impressions to be made throughout the school year, including Back-to-School-Night, parent/teacher conferences, staff meetings, plus new students enrolling mid-year.

Reciprocally, this insight on first impressions and the power of non-verbal communication should remind us to have grace and patience with students or others who might not make the best first impressions. This applies to *all* students, whether you teach kindergarteners, high school freshmen, 7th graders that act like toddlers, honors or intervention classes.

As a junior in high school, I made a horrible first impression on my English teacher and spent the rest of the year trying to convince him that I wasn't a complete clown. For weeks I focused in class and contributed to discussions in order to get back in his good graces, but I sure wish he'd given me a do-over on day two instead. Be purposeful with your first impressions and be forgiving with theirs.

Action Steps:

➢ **Stop to think about what you do and what you say on the first day of school. Based on this, what are the first impressions your students likely have of you?**

➢ **Are you forgiving when students make a poor first impression? Be prepared to give them fresh opportunities to make a good impression on you.**

Kids, Content, Both, Or Neither?
K-12 Perspectives

"What a teacher is, is more important that what he/she teaches." - Karl Menninger

"Kids before content. In my class, I don't teach English, I teach kids." - Unknown

Developing brains work in amazing ways. Swiss psychologist Jean Piaget's midcentury cognitive development theory defined stages of learning, which grow in complexity as we age. He found that from ages 0-2, infants learn about the world around them from senses and physical interaction. From 2-7, children start to understand basic concepts and symbols. From 7-12, they can begin to solve more involved problems using logic. And from 12 on, adolescents develop abstract thinking and work hypothetically and deductively (Piaget, 1958).

Perhaps Piagetian Theory and the way students learn helps to explain teacher grade level preferences or why we choose to teach what we teach. It has often been said that educators choose to teach elementary school because they love kids and helping them to develop skills and to solve problems. They choose middle school because they love both kids and content…or neither. And they choose high school because they love content and abstract thinking. Obviously, these are generalizations and exceptions are everywhere. There are, however, plenty of teachers that fit these typecasts. I'm sure you can think of a few.

To some degree the abovementioned stereotypes find their origins in another stereotype about students: that elementary students are enthusiastic and excited to learn; middle school students are curious, sassy, awkward, and impressionable; and high school students have largely made up their minds about the world and about how they learn. These are, of course, more generalizations. But there is some truth here as well.

Have the teacher stereotypes caused the student stereotypes or is it the other way around? For good or bad, students can influence the views of their teachers, and teachers can do the same for their students. Seeing as this is a book for teachers, I would encourage you to be the one actively and consciously doing the influencing. Show your students that you love them, that you love to learn, and that you love to see them learn and succeed. They are bound to follow your lead, even the older students who you think have already made up their minds about things.

So what? Now what? Take a moment to consider where you fit on this K-12 spectrum of stereotypes. Do you love kids, but find the curriculum content to be a drag? Are you enthusiastic about your subject, but your students make your job miserable? Whether you teach kindergarten, high school seniors, or somewhere in between, kids need to be supported and loved. There is no good reason why all teachers and all students should not be thrilled to geek out together.

So, if you don't love your students and your content, think about what you need to do in order to change that. If you already have a healthy love for both, consider how you might affect positive change on your school culture and how you might influence others around you to adopt a similar perspective.

Action Steps:

➢ **Take a moment to consider where you fit on the K-12 spectrum of stereotypes.**

➢ **Ask yourself where can you increase your enthusiasm: for students, for content, or both?**

The First Week: Build A Culture Without Wasting Time

"It's the first day of school. Teachers, put on your capes." - Unknown

"No significant learning can occur without a significant relationship." - James Corner

Many teachers focus on culture-building during the first days of school. For example, they may employ icebreakers, team-building, scavenger hunts, get-to-know-you games, classroom rules, and routines. These activities aim to ease anxiety, develop study habits, cultivate classroom ethos, or establish procedures. I knew one colleague who would spend four full weeks on this. He consciously gave up many instructional minutes in his math class in order to promote positive relationships with students. He would then make the most of the remaining 160 school days; he could push his kids to new heights because of the class culture he had established.

I have also experienced school-wide initiatives where "teach content on the first day" was the motto. This was instated to avoid using instructional time for procedures or other "fluff" during the first week of school. Since so many schools place an emphasis on high-stakes testing, it makes sense to take full advantage of the time you have with students. As far as we know, state testing is a necessary load that isn't going away anytime soon. Beginning in August, the days are numbered.

The need to tend to classroom culture collides with the need to dive into content. Both perspectives have their merit, and they don't necessarily have to be in opposition. There is a middle way. Take the get-to-know-you game, "Four Corners," as a case in point. This game presents a question with four options, requiring students to go to one of four corners in the room to signify their answer. The idea is that students not only reveal things about themselves, but they also get to see classmates with common interests. Instead of just asking questions like, "What is your favorite flavor of ice cream: chocolate, vanilla, strawberry or mint?" you could ask, "How do you like to learn: independently, in partners, in groups, or as a class?" In other words, culture-building games could incorporate questions that reveal learning modalities, cover classroom rules, identify leaders, frontload curriculum, informally assess, or do anything else that needs to be done.

Here are a few other ideas to blend culture-building and content. A scavenger hunt could require students to find items, locations, and information in the classroom related to both content and to routines and procedures. Students could form teams to contribute to a list of classroom rules, or a competition between teams of students could quiz them on classroom expectations, both of which also allow you to guide and model your own expectations for student interaction. The first writing assignment could be about students' strengths and weaknesses, about goals for their academic performance, about their favorite memories from the previous school year, or about their hopes, dreams, and expectations for this year.

The key here is to be thoughtful about culture-building activities and to do them with purpose or with multiple purposes. In the first days of school, not only can activities serve as culture-builders, they can also emphasize content and learning. Yes, a productive classroom culture is essential. Yes, instructional minutes are precious and should be used for teaching and learning. The good news is that there are plenty of ways to accomplish both at the same time.

Action Steps:

> **Consider how you can use the first days of school to both build culture and introduce content.**

> **Why do it?**

> **Is it enough time or too much?**

Bridging Worlds with
Cultural Responsiveness

"The best minute I spend is the one I invest in people."
- Ken Blanchard, One Minute Manager

"Culturally responsive teaching is the validation and affirmation
of the home culture and home language for the purposes of
building and bridging the student to success in the culture of
academia and mainstream society." - Sharroky Hollie

Buzz phrases can come and go in the world of education. Cultural Responsiveness is one that will last. In fact, Culturally Responsive Pedagogy (CRP) is simply a title for much of the good relationship-building and teaching that has been taking place in classrooms for generations. Basically, it's teaching that is considerate of students' backgrounds and builds trust between instructors and their pupils. Quoted above, CRP guru Sharroky Hollie boils it down to bridging the home culture with the school culture. Zaretta Hammond, another pioneer of CRP, says that, "Trust between teachers and students is the affective glue that binds educational relationships together." Columbia professor Christopher Emdin calls it an approach to teaching that "advocates for the consideration of the culture of the students in determining the ways in which they are taught."

CRP is powerful and transformative, but is also misunderstood. For one, CRP is not social justice or multi-cultural education, both of which can be valuable and impactful if done prudently. CRP is not a departure from "regular" teaching, nor is it an add-on set of strategies. It is not overgeneralizing: not all Hispanic families are from Mexico, not all people of African descent are African American, and there is no language called Chinese. CRP is certainly not *just* bringing in tacos on Cinco de Mayo, watching a Martin

Luther King speech in January, or doing an Eleanor Roosevelt lesson in March; all of which can be impactful learning opportunities.

No, CRP is something else, and it starts with knowing your students. Hammond claims that relationships with your students are really partnerships for the sake of learning, and she's right. In order to have an authentic learning partnership, you need each student on your team. They need to trust you and, whether it is verbalized or not, ultimately you need their permission to push them or to cognitively challenge them.

Humanize your exchanges, ignite positive emotions with your interactions, and establish trust through dependable two-way communication. Some teachers build trust by asking students about their lives and taking the time to get to know them. Other teachers connect with students through relatability, stories, humor, sarcasm, or silliness. Whichever methods you use to build trust, neuroscience connects powerful trusting relationships to meaningful brain development (Bornstein, 2012). So, go ahead and ask them about their game or recital over the weekend. Let them know how excited you are to introduce them to fractions and how often you use them in real life. Invite them to brainstorm with you as you plan a fun activity. Before long you'll see that when you practice CRP effectively, you will unleash powerful synergy in the classroom, and you and your students will become a team that struggles and succeeds together.

Action Steps:

> **Informally assess your student relationships by answering these three questions:**
> **Do you know your students well enough to partner with them in their learning?**
> **Do they thrive and enjoy the learning process in your class?**
> **Have they given you permission to push them?**

➤ If you answered "no" to any of these questions, then make it a point to get to know your students and earn their trust as you become more culturally responsive.

Want to Impact Students? Notice Them!

"Effective teaching is not a simple matter of executing specific behaviors and strategies, because effective teaching is grounded in human relationships" - Robert Marzano from Managing the Inner World of Teaching

"Kindness is the language the deaf can hear and the blind can see." - Mark Twain

I was recently approached by the parent of a former student from several years prior. She paid me a compliment that I won't soon forget. "That was really amazing when you wrote that thank you note to my daughter. It's actually still on our fridge and we still talk about it." It's true, I occasionally write thank-you notes to select students who either overcame hardship, put in extra effort, or who set positive examples for others. Sometimes, I write one to a student who excelled beyond expectation. These notes say something like, "Dear Student, thank you for being such a great presence in my class. I really appreciate that I can always count on you to bring your best every day." Honestly, for me, the practice of writing notes had become somewhat ordinary and routine. This encounter was a reminder of how powerful a teacher's words can be.

Even for the most challenging students there are opportunities for teachers to report on something positive. All students can have good days, good moments, slight improvements, or something bigger. Therefore, take the time to let them know that you see their successes. If you aren't a "thank-you-note" kind of person, send a message on their email or through your digital classroom, or call the student aside to let them know that you are thankful for them, that you care, or that you pay attention to their victories. Doing so will cultivate teacher-student bonds and strengthen your learning partnerships. It also serves as positive reinforcement for students who struggle with impulse control or who tend to test boundaries. The small amount of time and energy it takes to heap a little praise can reap mammoth rewards in terms of class culture.

In the same way, positive communication with parents is a brilliant practice to implement. A quick email or phone call to let a parent know that their child did something wonderful only takes a moment. This is especially handy when you might have to contact that same parent later with negative news. By that time, the parent already has had a positive first interaction with you and knows that you care about their child. Similar to positive notes or conversations with your students, positive parent contacts are a small investment of time that can generate a sizable return on investment.

My thank-you notes took a few moments to write and they had a powerful impact on individuals in my classroom. To at least one student, it meant the world. Chances are other students felt the same way. I needed to be reminded of that. So, Teachers, as of this moment you are hereby reminded as well.

Action Steps:

➢ **Make it a goal to connect with one student and one parent this week.**

➢ **Pick up the pen, the phone, or the keyboard, and let them know that you care.**

➢ **For the overachievers, make it a goal to connect with one student and parent each day this week.**

What Goes into A Lesson?
The Ideal Recipe

"A goal without a plan is just a wish." - Antoine de Saint-Exupery

Lessons come in all shapes and sizes. If you were to suggest that all good lessons must follow a rigid recipe, I would say that your thinking was limited. If you were to suggest that all lessons are good lessons, I would say your thoughts were much too broad. Effective lessons tend to have commonalities. Consider the following ten common ingredients that can be used in lesson design.

First, here are the disclaimers:

- Certain components are more essential than others.

- There are other pieces to consider that aren't listed here.

- The order may fluctuate.

- Other variables (e.g. school culture, grade level, content area, prior lessons) will impact lesson schemas.

- This list of ten is only meant to be a starting point for good lesson design.

- Sprinkle and mix in these ingredients and occasionally add others.

- Voila! You'll have yourself an ideal recipe for a lesson.

Ten common ingredients for lesson design

1. **Hook** - an attention-getter to draw students in or to connect to prior knowledge and interests. This could be a quote, activity, game, demonstration, short video, memory, joke, excerpt, cultural reference, statistic, something shocking, or any other thing that piques student interest in the lesson.

2. **Learning Objective**- a measurable goal or target for students to accomplish by the end of the lesson. This often starts with a phrase like, "students will…," "I can…," or "be able to…," followed by a verb (other than the verbs *learn* or *know*), followed by content or a skill that they didn't know or couldn't do before. For example, "students will determine the correlation between weight and speed by measuring falling objects" or "I can justify my position by using evidence from the text."

3. **Main Idea** - that which your students should focus on or come away with; the "big picture" for the lesson. This may be similar to the learning objective, but it is not to be confused with it. Some teachers state the main idea verbally, while others might write it on the board each day. It is vital that you state this early in the lesson, during the optimal window of learning (OWL) when students are most attentive, as well as later in the lesson. Examples of main idea statements include, "the area of a right triangle is one half base times height," or "The Declaration of Independence is really a breakup letter with England."

4. **Background Information** - material that students will need in order to accomplish the learning objective. This not only includes physical materials such as texts and handouts, but also portions of lecture or direct instruction. Direct instruction can be a valuable part of a lesson, but it is not the same as "delivering a lesson" and it is certainly not the lesson itself.

5. **Modeling** - teacher demonstrating what is expected of students. A clean model where the teacher walks through a sample problem and/or models expert thinking in order to set up a successful transition before releasing students to work. Whole-part-whole could come into play here, meaning the skill is demonstrated in its entirety, broken down into its parts and practiced, then put back together again.

6. **Checking for Understanding** - systematically measuring whether students are getting it or are ready to move on. CFU or formative

assessment can be done in many ways, from whiteboards and Chromebooks, to randomized calling or surveying the room.

7. **Gradual Release of Responsibility** - the transition from teacher control to student control of the responsibility of the lesson. Typically, GRR can go from a teacher model, to group work, to partner work, to independent work, checking for understanding at each step. Content could also increase in complexity at each step.

8. **Independent Practice** - the portion of the lesson when students are applying skills or knowledge to complete tasks without direct teacher support. To use math as an example, this would be a time when students demonstrate knowledge/skills to complete problems on their own. If CFU and GRR are done well, students will be successfully practicing skills and applying knowledge on their own.

9. **Assessment** - measuring student knowledge, skills, or accomplishments. Lessons won't always need a formal assessment like a quiz, test, or exam at the end. Assessing students can be done informally as well, depending on your needs. Formative assessments should be taking place throughout the lesson.

10. **Closure** - revisiting the goals for the lesson (i.e. the learning objective and main idea). This might include an additional checking for understanding or task for students to complete, such as a quick-write or an exit ticket.

Action Steps:

> **Consider your basic lesson design.**

> **Is there something major missing in your recipe?**

> **Introduce (or reintroduce) important elements to your next lesson.**

> **Do you regularly address all these elements?**

> **Pick one to improve on this season.**

Do Students Work Harder Than You? They Should!

"It's not the load that breaks you down, it's the way you carry it." - Lena Horne

I remember facilitating Jeopardy review games each unit during my inaugural year of teaching seventh graders. I prided myself on being youthful, innovative, and full of energy. Ego aside, I was wiped out at the end of a Jeopardy review day! I realized that I was working much harder than my students, feeling a bit like a referee who officiated youth basketball games all day.

As a matter of fact, I worked harder than *most* of my students on *most* days. And that is not something to be proud of; rather it exposed my naivety and signaled that I needed to make some adjustments. Whether it was direct instruction, monitoring progress, or grading assignments, I was wearing myself out. My students loved my class partly because I didn't expect much of them. I designed the lessons, I maintained control the whole time, I did most of the analyzing, I broke down the concepts, and I asked and answered most of the questions. Frankly, I did all the work. My students were satisfied having me serve as their entertainment, but I didn't push them, guide them, or hold them accountable to work hard or think deeply.

Thankfully, I wised up. I found that students can love the classroom experience and work their tails off at the same time. Even review games can encourage students to work hard, allowing you to be the facilitator, but not requiring you to drain your battery as the power-source of the lesson. The teacher should leave the room each day with a healthy sense of satisfaction. And just like a great workout, students should leave the room with a healthy and appropriate feeling of exhaustion, having been engaged in learning and building stamina to do even more going forward.

Some easy ways to do this include:

- setting and maintaining positive behavior expectations

- creating a classroom culture of loving the work

- embracing struggle or failure as a natural part of the process of growing and learning

- using structured student interaction and flexible grouping effectively

- authentically checking for understanding and letting these informal assessments determine lesson direction

- differentiating instruction to challenge all students, and delegating work to all students.

Action Steps:

➤ **If you are overly exhausted at the end of the day, determine whether it is related to how hard you work as compared to how hard your students work.**

➤ **If your students aren't working harder than you, they should be. Make necessary adjustments to lessons, directions, routines, or expectations to ensure this is the case.**

"Own" Every Lesson: Spice It Up with Your Own Flavor

"Seek first to understand, then to be understood." - Stephen Covey

Early in my career, I leaned heavily on colleagues for lesson-planning. I wouldn't have had an adequate curriculum without their help. The synergy made possible by collaboration continues through a teacher's career, but in the early years it is imperative if you want to thrive, not just survive. Years later in a new district with a completely new assignment, I spent many evenings piecing together lessons so that I could lead a group of students the next morning and avoid looking foolish or unprepared in the process.

Perhaps your experiences were similar or perhaps you are experiencing this right now. Whether you lean on other teachers, stick closely to a textbook, research online, or find downloadable curriculum, nothing works as well as owning your lessons. By "owning" I don't necessarily mean that you created it from scratch or have patents or copyrights on it, but rather that you have scrutinized and adjusted the lesson so that it is has become uniquely your own.

From textbooks, graphic organizers and worksheets, to activities, projects and documentaries, teachers have used all sorts of resources to develop curriculum. Nowadays, collaboration is common in departments and grade levels, and downloading lesson plans from "edupreneurs" (educational entrepreneurs) has become normalized as well. By all means, beg, borrow, download, or purchase lessons. But then *own* them. Don't leave them unexamined. Go through them with a fine-tooth comb. Break it down and build it back up. Spice it up with your own flavor. Make it better. Tweak, add, delete, and adjust. Make the lessons distinctly and unapologetically *yours*. When you own your curriculum, you are bound to teach with more confidence, more passion, and more energy. Your students will notice and flourish as well.

Action Steps:

> ➤ Modify an upcoming lesson in a way that excites you and will make you look forward to teaching it.

> ➤ Modify an upcoming lesson in a way that will excite students and have them on the edge of their seats

Tips to Transcend Classroom Management Issues

"Teach students how to do things right, don't just establish consequences for doing them wrong." - Doug Lemov

Being an effective manager of your classroom means having student behavior in check, but it doesn't necessarily mean being a harsh disciplinarian. Depending on the discipline policy at your school, you could go an entire school year without handing out so much as a detention. Don't get me wrong, there are behaviors that warrant appropriate consequences. However, if you implement other management practices in your classroom, you may not have to go there with your students very often. Here are five proven approaches to classroom management that don't focus on being strict or dishing out discipline. These approaches aren't about a teacher's response to questionable student behavior, but rather they aim to transcend the problem by nipping it in the bud.

Showing respect to your students is good classroom management. This is even true when they don't deserve it. In fact, it is especially true when they don't deserve it. Most students will naturally respect you in return. Keeping in mind that students can come into my classroom with all sorts of baggage, I have countered insolence with patience on a number of occasions. For the sass and attitude that may come your way, you can remind these students that you have always been fair, kind, and respectful to them. Your students won't always be motivated to behave because of school or classroom rules, they will behave because you are you; a teacher who loves, cares for, and treats them with respect.

Holding students accountable is good classroom management. There is an old saying that "teachers should not smile until Thanksgiving." Pure boloney! But it *is* true that you should not let behaviors go unaddressed.

This doesn't always mean consequences, but it could mean losing privileges, or talking with a student after others dismiss. As far as student accountability goes, do it early and often. Be firm and fair. Otherwise, your warnings will not hold any weight, unintentionally training students that actually certain behaviors are accepted. As a result, you will then spend a great deal of energy throughout the year trying to correct it.

Getting parents on board is good classroom management. Schools can't rely on all parents to raise upstanding citizens, nor can parents solely rely on schools to meet their children's every academic need. Remember that it takes a village to raise a child, and parents are arguably the main part of the village team. If an old-fashioned consequence doesn't do the trick to correct behavior (detention, sitting out of activities, losing recess, etc.), communicating with parents often will. When parents are aware of behavioral concerns, they have the opportunity to help you by holding their children accountable at home (with incentives, loss of privileges etc.). Parents can help; communicate with them.

Having routines and consistency is good classroom management. If students know what to expect at certain times of the day, what is expected during transitions, or what to do next when they finish a task, you are less likely to have to address poor behavior. Also, stand still and wait for attention before talking, otherwise you send a message that your words aren't important; not even to you.

Having a well-planned lesson is good classroom management. If your lessons are sufficiently engaging and relevant, you are less likely to experience students acting out. If students are having fun, being challenged, or both, they won't have time to engage in or even think about off-task behavior.

Respect, accountability, parent awareness, routines, and engaging lessons will mean that discipline episodes will be fewer and farther between. Classroom management is a necessary element to minimize distractions and to allow learning to occur. Of course, you may need to lay down the law from time to time. Nonetheless, you will have made discipline an ancillary issue, not the main issue.

Action Steps:

- ➤ **Examine your approach to classroom rules.**
- ➤ **Do you teach students to do what is right, or establish consequences for when they do something wrong?**
- ➤ **How would your students answer this question?**
- ➤ **Without considering traditional discipline, how can you improve your classroom management this year?**

Perspectives: The Balcony Vs. The Dancefloor

"...The only way you can gain both a clearer view of reality and some perspective on the bigger picture is by distancing yourself from the fray...If you want to affect what is happening, you must return to the dancefloor." - Ronald Heifetz and Marty Linsky

In *Leadership on the Line*, Ronald Heifetz and Marty Linsky make a compelling case for educational leaders to maintain a balanced perspective. They use a dancefloor metaphor, urging leaders to have both a holistic view from the balcony as they watch the dance, and to have a close-up view as they join in the dance. This metaphor is useful not just for administrators. Teachers formally lead in their schools and districts, and all teachers are leaders in their spheres of influence; namely, with the students in their rooms.

Teachers may err in either direction, missing the balanced perspective. For instance, you may work your tail off circulating the room and helping needy students, but miss the fact that most students are finished, bored, or off-task. Or you may sit behind your desk observing a collectively on-task classroom, but never pull up a chair and guide the academic discussions that ought to be taking place. You don't know because you're not down in the trenches with students.

Here's the simple takeaway: leadership in the classroom is multi-dimensional. To best lead students, you must get down and dirty from time-to-time. Literally get to their level. Pull up a chair. Not only will you be able to dialogue with students, getting to know how they think, and better addressing their needs, but you will have a profound impact on classroom climate as you build rapport. In order to best lead, you must also have a balcony perspective of your class, reading and guiding the class and based on collective needs and progress. Ultimately, you make the decisions to slow down, to dig deeper, to transition, or to move on. You set the tone, both from the balcony and from the dancefloor.

Action Steps:

> ➤ Avoid erring in either direction as you lead a classroom.
> ➤ When do you get lost on the dancefloor, losing sight of the big picture? When do you stay on the balcony, being disconnected from the learning process?

Dated, Dull, And Detrimental:
The Sage on A Stage

"Fortune and glory, kid. Fortune and glory." - Indiana Jones

"It is easier to judge the mind of a man by his questions rather than his answers." - Pierre Marc-Gaston

Students asking questions is a crucial part of developing knowledge. One study found that the average teacher asks over 300 questions to students each day, yet the average student asks only one question to their teacher every week (Graesser & Person, 1994). This is largely thanks to the centuries old Western educational model that exalts the teacher as the keeper of wisdom, the all-knowing professor: the sage on a stage. Wiktionary defines sage-on-a-stage as "an educator, especially at the post-secondary level, who imparts knowledge by lecturing to an audience." There are reasons why this method has been in vogue since the first European universities emerged in the Middle Ages. There are also reasons why the educational pendulum has been swinging away from this approach ever since.

Specifically, in the world of social sciences, sage-on-a-stage has worked for centuries because people enjoy stories. It's the reason we *like* things and *follow* people on social media. It is why movies will never go out of style. It's what drives us to binge-watch on Netflix. It explains Indiana Jones and his day job as a professor of archeology. Teachers of history are in a unique position since history is about stories, and children (even adults) are hard-wired to enjoy stories. And sages-on-stages can be found across content areas and grade levels, as well.

In recent years, educational leaders have frowned upon the sage-on-a-stage, noting that the teacher often does the lion's share of the critical thinking, leaving student-engagement and questions largely optional. The saying, "it's my job to teach and your job to learn" cannot enter our classrooms if the goal is student learning. Instead, the saying should be, "it's my job to teach and it's my job to see that you learn." If they haven't learned it, you may have spoken some words on the content, but you haven't *taught* it. Merely lecturing, however good you may be, doesn't guarantee that students learn. With an increased focus on skills over content knowledge, and with easy access to information in the digital age, sages on stages are becoming dated. To many students, the constant talking can be dull. And if students aren't given chances to think critically for themselves, sages can be detrimental to student progress. The pendulum has swung away from teacher-led learning and toward student-led learning as students from early grades are expected to read, write, and talk about content with deeper complexity in the classroom.

However, it is possible for the teacher to capitalize on students' love of stories without being the sage-on-a-stage and doing all the heavy lifting or critical thinking for the class. Students might get the story in a variety of ways, including watching clips, listening to direct instruction, or reading together. There are lesson designs that beautifully blend the love of stories with a student-focused environment, including high rigor and high engagement. So, go ahead and use stories to your advantage, but design your lessons to focus on learning, too.

Action Steps:

- ➢ **Bring to mind an upcoming lesson during which you will likely do a fair amount of talking.**
- ➢ **How can you carve out space for student engagement during the learning segment?**
- ➢ **Outside of your speaking, how have you allowed space or time for students to digest or engage with the content?**

Pursue "Tweeners" (On Staff and In Your Classroom)

"The kind of teacher you will become is directly related to the kind of teachers you associate with. Teaching is a profession where misery does more than just love company—it recruits, seduces, and romances it. Avoid people who are unhappy and disgruntled about the possibilities for transforming education. They are the enemy of the spirit of the teacher." - Christopher Emdin

Whether this stereotype is a strength or a weakness, some teachers can be notoriously difficult to get in line. For better or worse, this stereotype persists all over the place. In some schools this is the exception. In others it's the rule. Thankfully, many educational leaders have written on this stereotype and have advocated plans to curb it. For instance, Anthony Muhammad's *Transforming School Culture* identifies four types of teachers as a way to address and overcome staff division and negativity. *Fundamentalists* are highly resistant to change. *Survivors* are just trying to get by. *Believers* are willing to get on board with a worthy initiative. *Tweeners* can be influenced by other groups and their loyalty can fluctuate. (Muhammad, 2009).

One of Muhammad's central points is for leaders in schools to focus on those pivotal tweeners. The fundamentalists and survivors can wear you out, each in their own ways, and the believers are already with you. Tweeners are the biggest bang-for-your-buck in terms of positively changing school culture. Muhammad's model is tremendously useful, offering a big-picture perspective on faculty dynamics and overcoming staff division.

Taking Muhammad's model a step further, a similar strategy can work in your classroom with pupils as well. My classes often had fundamentalists who resisted, survivors who struggled daily, believers who were always with me, and tweeners who were often on the fence. With great results, I applied Muhammad's logic by focusing on my tweeners. When I spent all my time on fundamentalists or survivors, I was exhausted and had little to show for my efforts. Spending all my time with the believers only maintained a status quo. By far, targeting the tweeners was the best investment. When I worked to get the tweeners on board, the fundamentalists and survivors came along, too. Before I knew it, I had an entire class on the edge of their seats ready to work for me. Just as you would with fellow teachers, build relationships with your tweeners. Go the extra mile to bring them along. It will be worth your efforts and the rest are bound to follow.

Action Steps:

- ➤ **Consider Christopher Emdin's quotation.**
- ➤ **Who are the colleagues with whom you are closest?**
- ➤ **Are they the enemy of the spirit of the teacher? If so, find different associations and influences on your staff.**
- ➤ **Consider Muhammad's model as it relates to students.**
- ➤ **Who are the tweeners in your classroom and how can you target these tweeners for relationship-building?**

Support All Students:
MTSS, PBIS, UDL, RTI...Oh My!

"If a child doesn't know how to read, we teach. If a child doesn't know how to swim, we teach. If a child doesn't know how to multiply, we teach. If a child doesn't know how to drive, we teach. If a child doesn't know how to behave, we teach?... Punish? Why can't we finish the last sentence as automatically as we do the others?" - Tome Herner (NASDE President)

The two, three, and four-letter acronyms in the above title can produce a wide range of reactions. To many teachers, these acronyms may be completely foreign. For some teachers, these frameworks set the tone and shape the practices for an entire teaching career, rightly aiming to behaviorally and academically support *all* students. Let's define each of these acronyms, provide context, and highlight the collective value that such frameworks can have on the career of a teacher.

MTSS - Something of an umbrella term for several other frameworks, the Multi-Tiered System of Support (MTSS) comprehensively addresses instruction, differentiated learning, individualized needs, and systems that support students' academic, behavioral, and social success. Tier 1 supports aim to reach most students (e.g. classroom rules, school initiatives, positive relationships), Tier 2 supports aim to reach some students (e.g. small group instruction, behavior contracts), and Tier 3 supports aim to reach a few students (e.g. 504s, IEPs, counseling).

RTI2 - Whereas RTI is "Response to Intervention," RTI2 is "Response to Instruction and Intervention." RTI2 is a multi-tiered process under the MTSS umbrella, focusing on systematic support for special education, English learners, gifted learners, and others. RTI2 is a fluid approach that includes levels of support such as reading or math interventions.

PBIS - Positive Behavior Interventions and Supports (PBIS) is a multi-tiered approach to support social, emotional, and behavioral needs, particularly targeting under-represented groups. PBIS principles include proactive approaches to discipline, explicitly teaching behavior, and flexible approaches for children. BPIS also encourages restorative justice and restorative practices involving victim, offender, and community members in the process of reconciliation.

UDL - Universal Design for Learning (UDL) aims to give students equitable access to a high-quality education through lesson design around flexible learning experiences. UDL embraces learner variability, recognizes and removes learning barriers, and promotes expert learners. Students need different ways to learn, are motivated by choices in their learning experiences, and benefit from having options for demonstrating mastery. UDL incorporates common approaches that would be found in G.L.A.D. strategies, studying learning modalities, or applying differentiated instruction. UDL takes differentiation a step further by not predetermining variations in content, learning processes, student products, and learning environments. UDL leaves room for students to practice metacognition, consider how they learn best, and apply choice to their learning.

Consider the development of some of these frameworks in a California context. California's 6 million students is more numerous than the entire population in at least 30 other U.S. states. Factor in the state's unparalleled diversity and it becomes clear why California schools regularly underperform compared to schools in the other 49 states. Achievement gaps persist in California school districts with regard to race, foster youth, special education, and poverty. Regardless of affluence, California schools have a history of disproportionately suspending minority and socio-economically disadvantaged populations. These are just a few examples why MTSS, RTI2, and BPIS have been statewide focal points in recent years. On the East Coast, UDL was born in Connecticut and embraced for many of the same reasons: addressing equity, designing lessons that support all types of students, keeping individuals from falling through the cracks.

Supporting all students through MTSS, RTI2, PBIS, UDL or similar approaches seems wonderful, yet many educators remain cynical. Why are there such strong negative reactions to some of these frameworks? Simply put, it is hard work to reach students that are hard to work with. Offering flexibility can threaten classroom routines, order, or teacher authority. Changing one's approach to teaching may blur lines, mislay accountability, or compromise high expectations.

In the old mindset, needy students were outsourced (intervention, 504s, IEPs) or behavior students were eventually "moved out" by unwavering progressive discipline. In the same way that the California "Three Strikes" law is largely viewed as a failed policy, rigid progressive discipline wasn't the best answer to correct student behavior in the state either. With a new mindset, these types of frameworks put supports in place to help struggling students find success. Working with hard students is hard work, but it is rewarding work. And it is as important as the work teachers do with gifted students, average students, or compliant students.

Action Steps:

> ➤ **Consider your mindset when it comes to working with challenging students.**

> ➤ **Which frameworks might help you to shift your approach and embrace the hard work of working with "hard-to-work-with "students?**

The Value of Being and Learning Outside

"I go to nature every day for inspiration in the day's work." - Frank Lloyd Wright

Being outside is healthy; plain and simple. My mentor teacher used to praise classroom teachers who, "let the kids play with dirt and stuff." It was gruff, short, and sweet, but he was right. Countless studies have linked daily exposure to the outdoors with healthy side effects (Harvard, 2010). These include weight loss, increased brain function, decreased symptoms of ADHD and hyperactivity, an improved immune system, better sleep, longer life, greater happiness, and more. These findings should not only give us pause regarding how we spend our leisure time beyond work, but also how we spend our teaching careers. Some teachers have the luxury of being outside more than others during their workday. For the rest of us, we must get a little more creative, not only for our students' health, but for ours as well.

For some of us, the seasons dictate when this is possible. When weather permits, there are all kinds of ways to get your class outside from time to time without disrupting the rest of the school or sacrificing control of your class. Start with clear behavioral expectations for your students and a green light from your administrator, and then plan a learning segment that can take place outside. For example, physics demonstrations can create opportunities for students to throw, launch, fling, or hurl all sorts of objects on a field. Art projects can incorporate natural materials found on a scavenger hunt. Mapping, geography, or storyboarding skills can be practiced with sidewalk chalk and asphalt. So can any graphic organizer, for that matter. Other tasks traditionally done with pencil and paper can similarly be completed with outdoor materials. Biology, botany, astronomy, physics, chemistry, trigonometry, geometry, and algebra all can be related to things and places found or observed outdoors at a school.

One outdoor activity that was memorable for my students was an SR-71 spy plane lesson in which I guided my high school history classes compete in a paper airplane contest after we learned about the Cold War.

One outdoor activity that was memorable for my students was the Cold War SR-71 spy plane lesson in which classes competed in a paper airplane contest outside the gym.

To make outdoor learning last longer, the concept of an "edible school-yard" allows students to cultivate vegetable or herb gardens. Or if you need a simpler method to take a lesson outside, then start with reading. Reading is universal, occurring across grade levels and content areas, and is perhaps one of the easiest activities to take outside. Basically, the idea is to implement engaging outdoor lessons that you can return to each year. If you haven't taken a lesson outside, now is the perfect time to plan one, bringing a breath of fresh air to your teaching.

Action Steps:

- ➢ **Plan at least a portion of a future lesson outdoors.**
- ➢ **Tell your students why you are doing this and tell them some of the many ways in which they will benefit from it.**
- ➢ **Think about frontloading of expectations and impact to other classrooms; and then go for it!**

The Warm-Demander:
Soft-Hearted High Expectations

"Everyone carries a bucket of water and a bucket of gas in life. A leader has learned to throw the right one at the right time." - Orrin Woodward

"There are teachers who without much fanfare take the students who others say can't - can't read great literature, can't do algebra or calculus, can't and don't want to learn - and turn them into scholars who can." - Doug Lemov

If I consider my own schooling as a child, I can think of a few teachers who were great at having high expectations. They came every day with a list of demands, graded hard, and disciplined harder, but they were cold and struggled to connect with students. In fact, many of my classmates feared or even hated these teachers, finding them frightening, callous, and unapproachable. Let's call this prototype the "cold-demander."

I can also think of a few teachers who had gargantuan hearts but struggled to have a firm line in the sand. They could never put their foot down and didn't know how to accelerate academically with their students. They were so nice, but they didn't always push me or my classmates academically, and they let us get away with far too much nonsense. Let's call this prototype the "warm-allower."

I'm sure many of you can think of examples of both cold-demanders and warm-allowers. Neither type is particularly effective in the classroom. The good news is that there is a fusion of these two prototypes that incorporates strengths while leaving behind the weaknesses. Enter the "warm-demander" prototype.

The warm demander is a teacher who is culturally responsive. The warm demander knows their students and their students know them. They push and push and push some more, yet the students don't resist. In fact, the students welcome it. The warm-demander is approachable and connected to students. Learners in the classroom of the warm-demander can't wait for the next challenge. They have learned to embrace failure, recognizing it is a necessary step on the road to triumph. The warm-demander is intuitive, reads the room, and steers the class accordingly. Students in the classroom of the warm-demander don't call their teacher strict, they call their teacher reasonable. They don't call their teacher mean; they call their teacher fair. She is not only fun, but relevant. He is not just excited about learning; his excitement is contagious. The warm-demander is a brilliant balance between high expectations and an understanding heart.

Don't be a cold-demander, your students will resist and resent. Don't be a warm-allower, your students will regret and rebel. Be a warm-demander. Yes, there are concrete examples, strategies, and blueprints to help you get there. But it's more about mindset than anything else. Believe in your students, gain their trust, and convince them that pushing them to new heights is not only what you want for them, but what they want for themselves.

Action Steps:

> ➤ **Examine where you fall on the warm-cold spectrum as well as on the demand-allow spectrum.**

> ➤ **How can you adjust in order to be connected and approachable (warm), while also pushing students and maintaining high expectations (demander)?**

The Undeniable Power of Routines

"Forty percent of teachers spend more time keeping order than teaching." - Lee Canter

"The most important day of a person's education is the first day of school, not graduation day." - Harry Wong

Lee Canter's assertion is staggering, and it should remind teachers that we can do a better job of establishing and maintaining routines in order to optimize learning during the school year. Harry Wong's claim should remind us that we cannot assume that our students know what we want them to do at any given time. We have to take the time to train them. Wong adds, "The number one problem in the classroom is not discipline; it is the lack of procedures and routines" (Wong, 1998). With that in mind, here are six areas through which routines can help turn your classroom a well-oiled machine.

Daily Class Greetings - Greeting your students with consistency each day accomplishes much at the same time. It builds rapport, establishes a physically and emotionally safe learning environment, and establishes an opening routine to your class, signifying that it's time to begin. This may involve shaking hands at the door, greeting the class from the front of the room, singing a little jingle, call and response with the class, or some combination of these ideas.

Expectations - Make sure students know what to do at given times, such as when they enter the room or finish a task. Harry Wong wrote that, "The most successful classes are those where the teacher has a clear idea of what is expected from students and the students know what the teacher expects from them." Untold swaths of time can be wasted when students enter the room waiting for direction. Similarly, the kids who tend to complete tasks before their peers and are unproductive with the extra time, or worse, they distract others from learning. Commonly known as "bell work," establish expectations for what students are to do when they enter the room. Establish similar expectations for early finishers. Have them start on homework, get out a book, compare notes with a partner, grab an enrichment handout from a designated location in the room, or choose from a menu of fixed options. There may be different expectations for different occasions. Early in the year, take the time to teach them to your students. It will save you and your students untold quantities of time in the end.

Pick a Pavlovian Spot - Whether it is at your desk, behind your podium, or next to the whiteboard, have a consistent place in the room from which you give instruction or address your students. Your students will learn to treat your words from this spot with reverence. If you are moving around the room or trying to multi-task when you talk to your class, they will quickly conclude that what you have to say isn't even that important to you, so it can't be very important to them, either.

Transitions - You might have a clap pattern, hand signals, a designated place on the board with directions, or next-steps listed via board, projector, or device. Don't get frustrated if all 30 students don't move as one from task to task. Some students take longer than others to put away or get out materials. So long as they know your expected routines for transitions, you can move along with the majority while a few students straggle behind. In any case, don't just have a plan for transitions that your students can expect, teach it, and practice it. Check for understanding and engrain it.

Student Breaks - Teachers perhaps save some of their strongest opinions for this topic. Bathroom needs, stretch breaks, and trips to the water fountain can be the bane of a teacher's existence. Primary grade teachers often have open bathroom policies for good reason. Some teachers hand out hall passes. Others want students to earn them. Perhaps you establish that your students shouldn't go during the first or last 10 minutes of class since it's so close to a break. It could be your pet peeve that students break during direction instruction. You might require students to stay after class, owing you the time for their water break. You may have outside-the-box accountability, where students answer a content question before you let them reenter the room. "Sure, you can go to the bathroom, Billy. But it's getting back *in* that could be an issue" (wink, wink). Maybe you teach 12th graders and they can come and go within reason. Or maybe you teach kindergarten and classroom accidents are very much a reality in your world. In any of these cases, save yourself the headache by communicating expectations early, often, and by reinforcing as needed.

Huddle Groups - A great way to routinely differentiate without skipping a beat is the huddle group. It requires establishing a culture where students are honest about their progress. The huddle group works wonders when most of the class is ready to begin with a task, and a smaller number of students needs additional guidance. You can ask students to self-identify when they need additional clarification, calling them to "huddle" with you instead of keeping the entire class on hold. Or the teacher can identify which students need clarification by circulating the room and putting distinguishing marks or colors on student papers. This also works well to address the needs of students returning from being called out of class or who return from an absence. "Overtime conversations" with students who need a bit more direction can be applied as well. Establishing huddle group routines will keep students flowing, even when they are working at variable paces.

Action Steps:

> ➤ **Which concept regarding structure and routines could you incorporate into your classroom?**

> ➤ **If you already incorporate all these concepts, where do you see the most room for improvement?**

Stability Sweet Spot:
Between Lazy and Workaholic

"You can't do a good job if your job is all you do." - Unknown

*"Taking care of yourself is being there for your kids,
like how on a plane, they tell you to put on your
oxygen mask first." - Gwyneth Paltrow*

Here is something that students may not understand: teachers are real people with real lives outside of school. They don't spend every waking hour correcting papers, crafting earth-shattering lessons, or scheming about how to make students' lives miserable. Teachers eat, sleep, go on vacations, run errands, work part-time jobs, and raise kids of their own. Sometimes, the life of a teacher is healthy and balanced. Sometimes it's not. Whether you are new to the profession (and susceptible to burnout) or a seasoned veteran (and susceptible to fatigue), I would suggest three areas by which to gauge balance in your life.

First, do you have balance between life at work and life at home? Are you able to put work down when you get home? Are you able to compartmentalize and turn off work? The word *workaholic* is overused and often misconstrued. However, teachers are notorious for putting in countless hours beyond their contracted days from 8am-3pm, reading and learning and on weekends, grading during holidays, or lesson-planning on summer break. Of course, there are times when work may have to come home (notebook checks, grading essays, getting supplies for activities, or the preparing progress reports). Certainly, mental work comes home with teachers as there are students, situations, and circumstances that can keep you awake at night. Cases in point, I tend to dwell on difficult situations in students' personal lives that come to my attention; I unofficially plan lessons in my head during my morning commute; and I still don't sleep well the night before the first day of school. But as a general rule, whether it means coming to school a little early or staying a little late, teachers should aim to finish "work-work" at work.

Second, do you engage in healthy hobbies? No one understands "work-hard-play-hard" quite like a teacher. How do you play? It has been said that people who engage in hobbies live longer. Carve out time for sports, activities, the outdoors, museums, art, music, gardening, traveling, board games, movies, community service, or any number of other hobbies. Make hobbies non-negotiables in order to maintain a healthy lifestyle and equilibrium in your life.

Third, do you have a supportive community? Humans are designed for relationships. Without people invested in our lives, we tend to wither away. Admittedly, we all have different lots in life. We are not all wealthy. We don't all have or want hundreds of friends. And we don't really get to choose our birth family. But everyone has the power to cultivate healthy relationships. Your support community should go beyond coworkers, but can certainly include them as well. Surround yourself with people who will listen to you, laugh with you, encourage you, and tell you what you need to hear…even when it's hard.

How are you doing in these three areas? Are you *really* able to step away from work? Are you sustaining rewarding hobbies? Are you surrounded by a community that builds you up? If your answer is "no" to any of these three questions, it might be time to regroup and make some changes. You will thank yourself later for doing it.

Action Steps:

- ➢ **Put work down when you leave.**
- ➢ **Don't check phones or email for a set period of time.**
- ➢ **Explore new hobbies, or revisit old ones.**

- ➤ Grab your bucket list and go somewhere new this weekend.
- ➤ Surround yourself with people that will build you up, can be honest with you, or both.

A Student Creed:
Why We Teach and Why They Learn

"In schools the main problem is not the absence of innovations but the presence of too many disconnected, piecemeal, superficial projects…we're over our heads." - Michael Fullan

"It is purpose that created us, purpose that connects us, purpose that pulls us, that guides us, that drives us; it is purpose that defines us, purpose that binds us." - Agent Smith (The Matrix)

At the core of Michael Fullan's critique is the need for unity and a common purpose in education. One of my former colleagues had a distinctive way of addressing the issue of purpose in his classroom, at least at it pertained to the subject of history. He would have all students chant the same line when they entered his history classroom. He would ask, "Why do we study history?" and they would respond, "To avoid repeating mistakes of the past and to appreciate other cultures." This happened every day, each period, without fail. Those students repeated the same thing 180 times in his class that year. At the very least, his students were far less likely to question the relevance of history classes. Some even referred to his mantra when they were enrolled in my class years later.

I loved it, and for the most part, I agreed with it. Now, if we're going to be candid, repeating it every day was probably overkill. Instead, I adapted my colleague's approach by posting his motto in my room, alerting students to it when it was necessary. It was a good motto and a good answer to the question of relevance. To be sure, posting a history student creed certainly cut down on the "who cares" and "why does this matter" type of questions that tend to emerge from apathetic learners each year. Being transparent with your students about the aim of your class has ancillary benefits as well, such as building teacher-student trust, framing student focus, training students to scrutinize their learning experiences, and encouraging students to always process information with a critical eye.

For your own classroom, use or modify the history student creed. A similar creed could be created for science, language arts, mathematics, physical education, art, music, or any other subject. It reminds, encourages, and focuses learning for your pupils. It gives students a purpose for learning in your classroom and allows them to apply it to future endeavors as well. And if you ever question your *own* role as a teacher, perhaps it will remind and encourage you as well.

Action Steps:

> ➤ **Apply a personalized version of the student creed before you start your next unit.**
>
> ➤ **Make sure your students know what they are going to learn and why.**
>
> ➤ **Make sure both you and your students have purpose.**

The "Fun" Test:
Is This Lesson Fun? Well, It Should Be!

*"In every job that must be done there is an
element of fun." - Mary Poppins*

"Good teaching is ¼ preparation and ¾ theatre." - Gail Godwin

I once observed a teacher begin his lesson with something like, "Alright, today's lesson is going to be pretty dry. But it's really important stuff, so make sure you pay attention." This teacher was well-liked by his students and was a solid teacher in many ways. To be honest, I understood his reasoning. His *in* with students was that they trusted him to bring the best, most relevant content and, therefore, he could get away with starting a lesson with this sort of comment from time to time. However, I couldn't help but conclude that his boredom disclaimer was unnecessary at best and harmful at worst.

I deeply believe that while all content is "important," I have yet to find a lesson in which there were not multiple angles to make it fun. When I lesson-plan, I always ask myself the question, "Is this lesson fun?" If I couldn't answer that question with an affirmative, I knew I still had work to do. My personal standard was that the final answer to that question could never be no. Whether it be the hook, a sense of humor, a correlation with a funny video, or little-known details that I could use to puzzle even the deepest thinkers, every lesson had to pass the fun test. If the content was particularly dry, I looked to other strategies, such as the way in which I involved students in the learning, in order to make sure the lesson passed the fun test. This could be as simple as having teams of students race each other to fill out the warm-up on the white board.

Another tactic I employed was to make sure that each unit was more exciting than the one that came before. I didn't like the thought of an exciting unit ending and a mediocre unit beginning, so I planned to make all units exciting. I got to the point where I could tell my students at the opening lesson of every unit, "Class, this unit is my favorite so far. I can't wait to go through it with you!" Sure, some would catch on and ask, "Didn't you tell us that last unit?" My honest response was, "Yes, and it was true when I said it. But now it's true again."

Ultimately, the secret to passing the fun test lies in the approach of the teacher. It is all about the mindset that you model for your learners. Students react to the energy coming from the teacher. If you are dragging through content that you can't stand, you can be certain that it is even worse for your students. If for no other reason, make it fun for yourself, too. This is the greatest profession on earth. Take advantage of every day and enjoy it. If you enjoy the process of teaching the content or skills, your students will notice and will be willing to go anywhere you want to take them instructionally.

Action Steps:

- ➢ **Add some fun to an upcoming lesson plan.**
- ➢ **Consider humor, statistics, games, demonstrations, culture references, or funny videos to help students connect with the content.**

Live for The Weekend...
And the Work Week as Well

"Far and away the best prize that life offers is the chance to work hard at work worth doing." - Theodore Roosevelt

"A man is a success if he gets up in the morning and goes to bed at night and in between does what he wants to do." - Bob Dylan

I worked with a wonderful school secretary who sent out a daily email with sub coverage lists, the school bulletin, and of course her freshly Googled memes. Often the memes were funny and were chosen based on the day of the week, holidays, pop culture, current events, or teacher jokes, for example. It was a cute idea and over the years, I began to notice overarching themes in her memes. The themes were mostly positive, save one. Unintentional as it may have been, one of the covert messages she was sending was "we live for the weekend." For me as a teacher, this was a slight to something I hold sacred.

Most educators officially work about half of the 365 days in the calendar year. 185 or so are workdays, and 180 or so are non-workdays including weekends, holidays, and from winter, spring, and summer breaks. Naturally, I enjoy my weekends and holidays as much as the next person. The motto "work hard, play hard" resonates with me. However, the collective message of the memes began to bother me. At the risk of sounding cliché, I still have to say it: *Carpe Diem. Seize the day.* Love your job and love your students. Put on your game face and bring your best each day. It's worth it and your students are worth it. Before you know it, your teaching days will be over, and you may profoundly miss the classroom. You don't want to leave this career unfulfilled. You don't want regrets.

Enjoy your time off and take full advantage of weekends and vacation time. Rest, play hard, or do both. But don't forget that you are part of arguably the oldest and most rewarding profession on earth. Enjoy it while you have it. Give it your full effort, work hard, get creative, have fun, and teach like there's no tomorrow. You will have no regrets in doing so. Throughout your career, live for the weekend, and live for your work week as well!

Action Steps:

➢ As a teacher, you have the greatest job in the world and an opportunity to directly impact lives. Not everyone has it as good as you do.

➢ Wake up on a workday and be intentional about having an attitude of gratefulness for what you get to do for a living.

➢ Wake up on a non-workday and be intentional about having an attitude of gratefulness for rest, relaxation, adventure, play, family, or anything else that you have the fortune to experience.

Differentiation:
What It Is and Is Not (DI 1 Of 5)

"Differentiation is simply a teacher attending to the learning needs of a particular student or small groups of students, rather than teaching a class as though all individuals in it were basically alike." - Carol Ann Tomlinson

The more I work with teachers, the more I realize that there is misinformation circulating regarding differentiated instruction. A common DI application in the classroom goes something like, "I sit the bright kid next to the one that needs help." This strategy may have some merit, but it is flawed and it is *not* differentiation. For one, strategic or flexible grouping goes beyond pairing a gifted learner with a struggling learner. For two, either student in the scenario is likely to have an awareness of what you are doing and may resent the strategy.

Another common DI application sounds like this, "I give more work to kids who finish early." Again, this strategy has pitfalls, and it is not differentiation. You may be punishing successful students with more work. Gifted students in your class will catch on to your ruse and work at a slower pace to avoid more work. If extra work is a privilege or enrichment opportunity, be cautious that it does not appear that you are punishing students who need more time to complete tasks.

In the most simplistic form, DI is about mixing it up for your learners, all of whom learn differently. This is vital to connecting with students, turning on their minds, and bringing out their best. Mixing it up is essential for different learners in the classroom. If you ask a DI guru like Carol Ann Tomlinson, she would emphasize that DI is about student-choice, routines, and variable learning approaches for your varied learners. In fact, there are at least four categories to frame the DI discussion, including: varied learning environments, and differentiating process, content, and product (flexible grouping being a potential fifth category). Each of these four categories will be addressed in turn.

Action Steps:

➤ Ask yourself how you differentiate instruction for your students.

➤ Make sure that what you think is differentiation really is differentiation.

Approaches to Differentiating Content (Di 2 Of 5)

"In differentiated classrooms, teachers begin with where students are, not the front of a curriculum guide." - Carol Ann Tomlinson

Leading thinkers on DI generally place DI strategies into one of four categories: content, process, product, and learning environment. Truly, each category has endless strategies and there are more ways to differentiate than there are students in your classroom. All learners have a unique set of backgrounds and interests on which a teacher can capitalize, if they play their cards right. Here are some fundamental concepts to start the conversation about differentiating content.

Differentiating "content" refers to varying what your students learn about. Have you ever used informational text that wasn't quite the right fit in terms of reading level? Why not offer different reading levels for the same piece of text? This is becoming much easier with the advent of web-based resources and some websites can do this free and automatically. In the same way, you could provide different groups of students with different versions of vocabulary lists, ranging in complexity based on student needs or abilities.

Based on informal assessment or feedback, it is likely you will recognize the need to further differentiate instruction as you identify groups of students who require more support or who need an extended challenge. Huddle groups would work swimmingly in this scenario. Try calling together a small group of struggling learners in order to reteach a concept while the rest of the class dives in. You could also call your small group of advanced learners who need an opportunity to extend their knowledge in order to challenge them with new direction. Or perhaps call the middle of the road students and evaluate them as your canaries to get a feel for the progress or mastery of entire class. The beauty with huddle groups is that your entire spectrum of students can be included from time-to-time, erasing the stigma that small huddle groups are only for struggling students.

These are only a few strategies to consider, drops in an ocean of content differentiation. Generally speaking, teachers can endlessly differentiate content based on indicators such as learner profile (visual learner, left-handed, 504 Plan, introverted, etc.), readiness (reading level, strengths, background knowledge, etc.), or interest. Sometimes even when a task is challenging, students will compensate if their interest is high enough. Any student with interest and access to content is on track for an effectual content-differentiated learning experience.

Action Steps:

> ➢ **Ask yourself how you differentiate content for your students.**
> ➢ **How could you incorporate strategies such as varied reading levels or huddle groups based on learner profile, readiness or interest?**

Approaches to Differentiating Process (Di 3 Of 5)

"That's at the core of equity: understanding who your kids are and how to meet their needs. You are still focused on outcomes, but the path to get there may not be the same for each one." - Pedro Noguera

Leading thinkers on DI generally place DI strategies into one of four categories: content, process, product, and learning environment. Students have different learning modalities and learners process information differently. Here are some thoughts to get you started in terms of differentiating process.

Differentiating "process" refers to changing up how students practice skills or learn content. For instance, using activities with divergent tiering, varied levels of support, or increasing complexity are ways to cover the same basic skills with all students. To do this, you could require all students to cover the anchor activity or "work in common," and pair this requirement with "other work" in order to meet individual needs. This "other work" could be of the teacher's choosing or the student's, and could be based on interest, ability or both.

Other popular strategies to differentiate the learning process are the use of manipulatives, hands-on support, or allowing varying lengths of time for task completion. One of my personal favorites is the "gallery walk," which serves to differentiate the content and the process at the same time. In a gallery walk, the teacher presents visual/textual information on different topics or from different sources around the room, such as primary sources, pictures, text, artifacts, etc. Students report on a certain number of items of their choosing. In doing so, they are able to focus on multiple areas of interest while being exposed to different ways of organizing information.

Process differentiation can go in several directions. Some learn by hearing or seeing, some by discussing or organizing, and others are hands-on.

Ensure that the process by which learning occurs in your classroom caters to all your learners.

Action Steps:

> ➤ How can you differentiate student learning processes?
> ➤ How could you provide varied levels of support, common work, student choice, or gallery walks?

Approaches to Differentiating Product (Di 4 Of 5)

"Plan to be better today, but don't ever plan to be finished." - Carol Ann Tomlinson

Leading thinkers on DI generally place DI strategies into one of four categories: content, process, product, and learning environment. Offering students choices in their learning is one of the most powerful ways to optimize instructional time and to engage and push your students. Student choice can be accomplished in differentiating content and process as well, but is relatively straightforward when applied to product. Here are some ideas to differentiate what students produce.

Differentiating "product" refers to the various ways that students might produce work to demonstrate understanding or mastery. To begin, you could require students to produce the same work but apply adjustable rubrics, which address the varied skills in the room. You could also mix up or offer choices regarding whether students work individually, in partners, or in groups. You might also consider offering open-ended tasks (within teacher-determined parameters).

When it comes to culminating activities or assessments, it does not always have to be a traditional test or writing assignment. Instead of having all students take an exam or write an essay, you could allow them to pick from a menu of possibilities. Alternate products might be writing a letter, drawing a picture, singing a song, creating a storyboard, or making a slideshow or video. If you are set on traditional assessments, then allow students to choose an alternative product to demonstrate mastery for partial credit.

Ultimately, students can show you what they know in any number of ways. The product should be the fun and engaging part. Lay out options and let them show you what they know in a way that works both for you and for them.

Action Steps:

> ➢ Ask how you differentiate what students can produce.
> ➢ Beyond traditional tests, how could you design innovative ways for students to demonstrate mastery?

Differentiating Learning Environment (Di 5 Of 5)

"We don't get to decide whether we have challenging students in our classes, but we can certainly decide how we respond to them." - Carol Ann Tomlinson

Leading thinkers on DI generally place DI strategies into one of four categories: content, process, product, and learning environment. Flexible grouping and adjustments to the learning environment can provide all sorts of options for independent and collaborative learning. Here are some ways to use the learning environment as a tool to differentiate.

Differentiating the "learning environment" refers to varying settings in which your students work. This could include physical locations in the room, throughout the school, or a place at home where students can work quietly, have access to technology, or are encouraged to collaborate. For virtual learning, this perhaps even more imperative since students need a quiet or productive workspace designated for their school work.

Also, establish a culture that invites different types of learners. For instance, design your classroom as a place conducive for all students to learn, from those who might need to move around the room, to those who might need a quiet place to sit and work independently. Classroom materials or settings might also reflect various cultures or home settings to differentiate the learning environment.

Perhaps most importantly, learning environment differentiation is optimal when the teacher has clear guidelines for transitions and independent work. When the teacher is occupied and students need assistance, established routines should be in place to optimize instructional time. Flexible grouping, where desks are ready to quickly transition from rows, to partners, to groups, can also be used advantageously in this context.

A classroom with rows or groups of desks is common, but it is not the only way to learn. Pay attention to your students' learning needs. Give them options and guidelines as you mix up the settings in the classroom. The need for social distancing in the classroom presents a distinct challenge to learning environment differentiation as schools balance effective learning with the need to keep students safe and healthy. How do teachers encourage interaction and collaboration when students must stay physically distanced and stationary?

Specific to virtual instruction, I have observed teachers effectively engage students by having them to create active spaces at their desks, to scavenger hunt around their homes, to build towers with household items, or otherwise learn kinesthetically through Google or Zoom meetings.

Regardless of the setting, the possibilities are endless for learning environment differentiation. Whether traditional classroom teaching, hybrid teaching with smaller class sizes, or providing virtual learning, consider how to use varied learning environments to best involve students.

Action Steps:

➢ **Ask yourself how you vary setting or learning environment to allow all students to succeed.**

➢ **How are seats arranged to quickly change settings if necessary?**

➢ **How can the high energy students move around and get their wiggles out?**

➢ **How can those that need focus find a quiet spot?**

Want to Improve? Do What Works

"If you can't explain it simply, you don't understand it well enough." - Albert Einstein

There are many influential names in education; few are bigger than Robert Marzano. In *What Works in Schools: Translating Research into Action*, Marzano highlights areas of focus in a straightforward way that lives up to the book's title. He boils it down to five topics, ordered by most influential in terms of achieving academic improvement in schools.

When you take his list of five into consideration, you will see that they apply to both the school at large, as well as the individual classroom. Not to be confused with Marzano's *Classroom Instruction that Works*, which looks at specific applications for a number of research-based strategies, these are Marzano's ideas for school improvement as applied to the classroom (Marzano, 2003).

Guaranteed and viable curriculum - This is the greatest indicator for a successful school. Unfortunately, some schools can't promise all students access to a practical curriculum, often because they can't staff properly credentialed teachers or they already have teachers who are ineffective. If students don't all have access to the same content, knowledge, and skills in every classroom, it will be extremely difficult to equitably move students forward. Additionally, schools must provide and protect instructional time for their teachers to do the work of providing this curriculum to their students.

Challenging goals and effective feedback - High expectations are essential for improving student achievement. If you set a low bar, students will jump over it, but usually won't jump any higher than they must. Many more will rise to the occasion if you set a higher bar. Offering effective feedback to students is also a non-negotiable. Providing this feedback presumes that you are monitoring student progress and adjusting instruction accordingly.

Parent and community involvement - This includes establishing mediums for communication such as home visits, a school website, parent access to digital classrooms, recorded phone messages, parent-teacher conferences, or norms for parents to communicate with teachers. It also includes parents and the community being a part of the day-to-day running of the school, such as volunteering in classrooms, guest lecturers, Open House, or attending PTA or School Site Council meetings.

Safe and orderly environment - Schools and their classrooms must have effective plans to keep students safe and preserve order on a campus. This topic has been given greater attention in recent decades with the prevalence of school shootings and a subsequent focus on lockdown procedures and active shooter drills. But a focus on student safety doesn't just mean physical safety, but a school must also maintain an atmosphere conducive to learning, which includes addressing student behavior. This suggests a productive school climate or positive school culture. If distractions are curtailed, students can go about the business of learning.

Collegiality and professionalism - Teachers interacting in a positive way to promote and support student learning is hugely important in schools. Moreover, teachers should be part of a shared vision, have shared goals, and be a collective group that learns together. Staff professionalism sets an example and sets a tone for the greater school climate.

Action Steps:

- ➢ **Using the Marzano checklist, weigh in on the work you do.**
- ➢ **Do your students have access to all the necessary curriculum?**
- ➢ **Do you give your students challenging goals and effective feedback?**
- ➢ **Are parents and/or community members involved in the learning?**
- ➢ **Do you provide a safe and orderly environment?**

- ➤ Do you regularly model collegiality and professionalism in order to promote student learning?
- ➤ Furthermore, how could you promote change related to these concepts outside of your classroom, such as at a site or district level?

What Goes into A Unit?
How to Mix an Ideal Recipe

"Start with the end in mind." - Stephen Covey

A unit can mean different things to different people. It can range from a few lessons to dozens of lessons. The series of lessons are tied together by a common theme. A unit might utilize slideshows, devices, research, activities, tasks, image or video analysis, a series of problems, or creating a product. Regardless of how long the unit or how you choose to develop it, keep in mind these three universally applicable tips.

Backward planning - Also called backward design, backward planning designs a unit based on the final goal. When the goal is standards driven, this type of unit can be called a "standards-based unit of study" or SBUS. If you want students to meet certain standards or to answer certain questions on a unit exam, then you start with the material on your exam when you go about planning the unit. If you want students to generate a final product, to demonstrate a set of skills, or to organize information by the end of the unit, the lessons leading up to that objective should prepare students to succeed. A unit makes much more sense with the end in mind.

Looping information - Consider an art unit that looks at works from a dozen famous artists in sequence. Now imagine a math unit that presents several different skills and has students apply the skills to solve problems in a culminating activity. Depending on the content, student learning can be quite linear (like the art unit), or can build in complexity (like the math unit). Let's consider a history unit next. The lessons of a history unit might be linear, such as a chronological overview of major occurrences within a larger historical event. The lessons might also build in complexity as causes and effects often intertwine, and as there are conflicting perspectives and interpretations of events. Either way, you are able to loop the information as you go. Looping (also called spiraling) is more than just review, it is about highlighting connections that exist throughout the content. For a linear unit, looping means revisiting content ("Hey, remember when we learned about Van Gogh's style? I'm noticing Monet has a similar style, but with more pastel colors instead of bright ones"), and for a more complex unit, looping means resynthesizing content ("You already know how to find the area of a triangle and a rectangle separately. Now apply these skills to find the area of this new shape that looks like a triangle on top of a rectangle"). This practice will prepare students for a final assessment, demonstration, project, or task as they work through the connections throughout the unit.

Formative assessments - Also known as informal assessment or checking for understanding, formative assessments refer to the ways in which you measure student progress. You should be monitoring their progress and giving timely feedback. Formative assessments work to gradually prepare students to succeed with whatever it is you expect them to do by the end. Unless you want to be behind the eight ball when students are expected to perform at the end, consistent effective feedback for students is a necessity.

Sprinkle a little slideshow, list a few key terms, develop a graphic organizer or two, sneak in a primary source, get your devices ready, plan the activities, prepare them for a final activity…and voila! You have yourself a unit. Just don't forget to plan with the end in mind, to loop information, and to check their understanding along the way.

Action Steps:

- ➢ **Before you begin your next unit, be sure that you aren't simply going from one lesson to the next, hoping students remember it all by the end.**

- ➢ **Start with backward planning, deliberately looping information, and use formative assessments to allow students to practice and build skills before the final test or task.**

Get Out to See Your Fellow Faculty at Work

"You are never too old to set another goal or to dream a new dream." - C.S. Lewis

Teaching should not be done in isolation. Many teachers are the lone adult in a room most of the day, while others may co-teach, work with aides, or have parent volunteers. In any case, don't be a silo in terms of your collaborative work with colleagues. As often as you can, get out of your room and soak up the wisdom around you. This can be accomplished in a virtual environment as well, which could mean joining virtual lessons to see colleagues in action with their students.

Around year two or three of classroom teaching, I was confident in my classroom management and lesson-planning. I was capable of "cruise control teaching" much of the time. But I wanted to be better for my students; I *knew* I could be better. I knew that some of the answers were in books or professional development, but answers were also all around me at my school site. During my one-hour prep period each day, I would make a habit of watching a nearby teacher deliver instruction. His lessons on the Aztecs blew me away. He shared details about the social hierarchy, about the use of specialty weapons, about gruesome rituals and more. I couldn't get enough of it. And though I wanted to, I could not teach it exactly like him. In addition to what I learned in his classroom, I also learned from the observation process. I learned that I needed to see certain strategies and pedagogical approaches, digest and adjust them, and make them my own.

I went outside my department as well. One math teacher comes to mind. He and I could not have been more dissimilar in our teaching styles. He was a veteran in the twilight of his career, soft-spoken, and his classroom felt very serious and focused. He used call and response cues that I thought at the time were too childish for me. But his students hung on his every word. They revered him. And ultimately, his students outperformed their peers in other math classrooms. As with my history colleague, I couldn't do what this math teacher could do, at least not how he did it. But I brought many ideas from his room to mine, adapted a few of his ideas, and found myself becoming a more effective teacher in the end.

Classroom visits in my early years lead to fruitful conversations, to previously untapped synergy, to personal growth, and to an overall more effective learning environment. Today, I still enjoy going to watch colleagues teach. I also recently noticed a colleague going out to observe other class-rooms. This was ostensibly peculiar since he was one of the finest teachers around, and was an educator with humility that, to be completely honest, should be visited by other teachers more often. But to him it was essential that he improve, a humble approach to his craft that is to be celebrated. No matter how well we teach, kids are always changing, and we can always be better for them. One readily available way to do this is to get out of your room and see what's happening around campus.

Action Steps:

> **List three teachers at your site that excel at their craft.**
> **Make a point to go watch them teach.**
> **And don't forget to have conversations with them afterward.**

I'm Watching Other Teachers Teach. What Do I Look For?

"Teachers are given an opportunity to experience the dissonance that exists between current and next practice. This dissonance is used as a catalyst to engage in meaningful reflection and purposeful action that supports progress toward expert performance." - Tony Frontier and Paul Mielke (Making Teachers Better, Not Bitter...p 233)

It's funny how educators can think alike. I had been observing teachers on my own for some time when I came across Frontier and Mielke's book *Making Teachers Better, Not Bitter*. In it, they offer similar advice for observations. Watching other teachers teach isn't an end in itself. It is a means to improve. This is a necessity for beginning teachers, but should also be a habit for seasoned veterans. Observing colleagues is not just a selfish pursuit as you look to get better, it will be better for your students, allow you to bring in more engaging lessons and introduce more effective practices. There may be some things you plan to observe that are difficult to grasp, in which case multiple visits could be in order. In any case, before you visit another teacher, get permission, tell them what you are looking for, and plan to debrief afterward.

Getting permission may be less of a necessity if you visit a close colleague, but you don't want to come in if you aren't welcome. Revealing your purpose narrows the focus and leads to a more purposeful and calculated visit. For example, let's say you are really interested in how to run a Socratic Seminar, and you've heard they have a unique approach to flexible grouping, or they are known for their formative assessment techniques. After observing the class, plan to have a follow-up conversation. Don't skip this step, because this is where the magic happens. Ask questions like those listed below. These conversations open the cooperative doors and cultivate collaborative relationships.

- "When you transitioned, what happened next?"

- "How did your students respond to that?"

- "I was intrigued by your strategy. What was your desired outcome?"

After you have laid the foundation for your visit, what should you look for? You may want to watch a teacher with a group of students that are unknown to you. Or you may want to watch a teacher work with students that you share during the school day. Either way, consider at least five realistic outcomes from an informal peer observation:

- new approaches to teaching and learning

- adjustment of your rigor or student expectations

- new ideas of how to work with and manage the same students in your own classroom

- fresh appreciation for the work of cross-department, cross-grade-level, or cross-campus colleagues

- newfound acknowledgement of the hard work your students do in other classes throughout their day

Reading books and going to conferences can help you become a better teacher. But if you aren't careful and intentional about working with the people around you, teaching can be isolating. Don't forget that there is also wisdom at your school site. You have wisdom to share as well. Take the time to go and facilitate exchanges of wisdom. It doesn't have to be threatening, awkward, or draining. It doesn't have to last two hours. 5-10 minutes may be all that it takes to observe. Take the initiative to schedule it, to determine a focused intention for your visit, and to converse about it afterward. And as mentioned in the preceding chapter, don't let virtual learning deter you from the follow-up conversation. With a variety of formats such as email, text, or teleconference, it is now easier than ever to reach out to colleagues.

Action Steps:

- ➤ Go watch another colleague teach.
- ➤ When you discuss with them afterward, have specific questions in mind and listen carefully as you let them do most of the talking.

Critical Thinking? Dive in With Webb, Bloom, Or Costa

"The function of education is to teach one to think intensively and to think critically. Intelligence plus character. That is the goal of true education." - Martin Luther King Jr.

What is critical thinking anyway? To engage in critical thinking means to become immersed in substantial intellectual pursuits. Some say critical thinking is thinking about your thinking while you are thinking it. It may last for a few seconds, several minutes, or hours at a time. If you look carefully, you might see smoke coming out of students' ears when it's happening.

Educators have treasured (Benjamin) Bloom's Taxonomy for decades (1956) as a way to classify learning into levels of complexity. (Arthur) Costa's Levels of Questions also challenged us to think about thinking and inquiry (1989). Then (Norman) Webb's Depth of Knowledge took 21st century education by storm (2002), offering a new tool to categorize tasks by complexity. And don't forget Higher Order Thinking Skills, a recent alternative to these three critical thinking paradigms.

With so many different models, how is critical thinking best measured in the classroom? Though I run the risk of oversimplification, I would suggest that they are all similar in purpose. Be it based on *Bloom's Taxonomy, Costa's levels of questions, Webb's depth of knowledge* or *higher order thinking skills,* the point is to get your students to think deeply about content, be given opportunities to explain their thinking and to practice skills. This doesn't mean that the teacher thinks critically while lecturing and trusts or hopes that students are coming along for the ride. It means teachers let *them* do the critical thinking.

A teacher needs to show them how to do these things, right? Yes, teacher modeling has its merit, but you cannot talk during the entire lesson and call it modeling. In fact, this may obstruct their critical thinking. Stop and let students draw conclusions without you doing it for them. This is where tools such as student interaction, gradual release of responsibility, and checking for understanding can come into play. For example, ask students to use their own words to describe their thinking on a math solution, or ask students to take a position and defend it with evidence. In any lesson, look for ways to create intentional moments in your lessons to let students think critically.

Action Steps:

> ➤ **Be it Bloom's Taxonomy, Costa's Levels of Questions, or Webb's Depth of Knowledge, make sure that your next lesson allows for opportunities for your students to think critically, not just you.**

Monkey on Your Back

"Great classrooms are characterized by positive, open relationships, mutual respect, and a shared responsibility for the learning process." - Robert John Meehan

"What is important is seldom urgent, and what is urgent is seldom important." - Dwight D. Eisenhower

If you haven't read "Management Time: Who's Got the Monkey?" it's relatively short and worth reading for anyone working in a professional setting. Originally printed in the Harvard Business Review in 1974, this classic piece on time management, delegation, and manager-employee relations is timelessly relevant. In short, the article suggests that a common corporate concern is that managers don't have enough time and their workers don't have enough work. This is the case largely because managers load metaphorical monkeys on their own backs, failing to communicate clearly, committing to the wrong tasks, and ultimately answering to their subordinates instead of the other way around. Although written with business managers in mind, the pearls of wisdom in this article are easily applied to teachers in the classroom.

In many ways, the teacher is the classroom manager and the students are the "subordinates," a politically correct term in 1974. Without realizing, students throw monkeys on the backs of their teachers, leaving teachers exhausted and confused. Consider these common student requests, and teacher responses.

- "Did you input the points for my assignment yet?"

    - Not yet, but I'll do it soon.

- "Why did I get that low of a score?"

    - I can take another look at it if you want.

- "When can I make up my test?"

- I can send a pass for you tomorrow.

- "I don't know what to do."

  - I'll be there in a minute.

In each of these scenarios, students are holding out a monkey and the teacher is willingly placing it on their own back. In the final analysis, the teacher has not established boundaries and is left to answer to the student in each situation. Sound familiar? I hope not.

Instead, the teacher response should communicate that the onus is on the student. For instance, consider where the monkey lands with these responses.

- "Did you input the points for my assignment yet?"

  - I plan to enter grades at lunch tomorrow. If you notice I haven't updated yours by Wednesday, come check in with me.

- "Why did I get that low of a score?"

  - I'd love to talk to you about that. Can you come in before school tomorrow to discuss?

- "When can I make up my test?"

  - I have some students coming in after school tomorrow. Can you make it?

- "I don't know what to do."

  - Talk to two classmates. When I come back in five minutes, have a specific question ready for me and I will happily help.

Better yet, have the foresight to put any of this pertinent information on the board. Then all you need do is point.

Notice that each response is kind and appropriate, yet each response encourages student responsibility, putting the monkey where it belongs. Sometimes it's suitable to bend over backwards for your students. But if you are enabling or conditioning a reliance on you, you are doing them a great disservice. And if you are facing migraines by day's end, you are doing yourself a disservice as well. Don't sabotage yourself by carrying their monkeys. Only allow the proper monkeys to climb on your back. Put the rest of the monkeys where they belong.

Action Steps:

> ➢ **List some students' monkeys that you tend to place on your own back.**

> ➢ **Plan out the appropriate words to say as you build capacity in your students, gently giving these monkeys back to your students.**

Take A Moment to Write A Proper Learning Objective

"Students who can identify what they are learning significantly outscore those who cannot." - Robert Marzano

Students may have personal goals to succeed in your class, but daily goals must go beyond "I want to get an A" in order to enhance learning. Some call it a learning objective, while others call it a learning target or learning goal. Some start with "I can" statements or "students will be able to…," while others start with the applicable verb: "analyze," "summarize," "predict," etc. The titles and specifics are not as important as the purpose. The learning objective isn't just an optional ingredient when planning a lesson, it is the main ingredient.

As Robert Marzano proposes, students should be able to identify what they are learning. Some teachers prefer to put an agenda or main idea on the board in place of a learning objective. There is nothing wrong with posting these things, but it is not sufficient and cannot replace a learning objective. There are times when a lesson goes on for multiple days, but most of the time learning objectives will change daily, and with each transition to a new subject in class.

The larger purpose of a learning objective is to set a goal for both the teacher and the student to measure their progress. John Hattie calls this "visible learning," a phenomenon where the teacher staunchly evaluates their own teaching and sees the learning process through the eyes of their students, helping them become their own evaluators (Hattie, 2015). If someone came in the room and asked an average student what they are learning, what would they say? When students go home and their parents ask what they learned in school that day, what would you want your students to say? What if someone asked you as the teacher about your class? Do *you* know what you are measuring in terms of student learning for any given lesson?

In practice, setting learning objectives isn't as daunting as it seems. Simply ask yourself, "What should my students know or be able to do at the end of this lesson that they didn't know or weren't able to do before?" By definition, the learning goal needs a verb. For example, instead of "American Revolution," you might write, "Students will summarize the causes of the American Revolution." Think of it this way, you can't measure "American Revolution," but you can measure whether your students can summarize its causes.

As a teacher, you can also determine how to proceed with the next learning goal based on your examination of student progress. In a very real sense, learning objectives are moving targets as your students advance and grow during the school year. You may find that a posted learning objective was met by all students, met by some, partially met, or not yet met. You may find that students have an awareness of the goal (good), a knowledge of the goal (better), or an understanding of the goal (best). Goals can and should be challenging for your students, meaning they often won't get there on the first try. This doesn't make you a bad teacher. Strive for progress, not perfection. The learning objective, *the* essential element of lesson design, allows you and your students to make that progress and measure and adjust accordingly.

Action Steps:

- ➤ **Look at an approaching learning goal and ask yourself the following questions:**
- ➤ **Can it be measured in terms of what students can do or know?**
- ➤ **Does the verb allow for enough critical thinking?**
- ➤ **Does the goal match what students are being asked to do?**

Social Emotional Learning, Trauma-Informed Practices

"All children have within them the potential to be great
kids. It's our job to create a great world where this
potential can flourish." – Stanley Greenspan

An alarming reality is that children who have experienced trauma are the rule more than then exception. And regardless of where you teach, or how wonderful your community is, you have students that have experienced trauma. According to the National Center for Mental Health Promotion, 60% of adults report having childhood trauma, and 26% of children experience trauma before they turn four (National, 2012). Trauma can be categorized as abuse (sexual, emotional, or physical), neglect (emotional or physical), or household disfunction (divorce, substance abuse, domestic violence, or incarceration or mental illness in the family). The CDC and other mental health organizations refer to each of these types of trauma as "adverse childhood experiences" or "ACEs." ACEs are often tallied, meaning a student with more ACEs has experienced more trauma. Districts everywhere are beginning to invest resources to address social-emotional learning (SEL), hiring non-academic counselors, therapists, and the like. And as we are about to see, teachers can be a large part of the healing process as well.

At school, students with ACEs are more likely to have reading deficiencies, lower grades, truancies, and discipline issues. These students tend to struggle with academic functions such as attention, memory, focus, organization, processing, and planning. These students also are more prone to have difficulty with authority, redirection, or criticism, and may struggle with depression, substance abuse, or self-injurious behavior (Morgan, 2019).

There is hope, however. A recent study out of San Francisco suggests that "benevolent childhood experiences" or "BCEs" can counteract or even help overcome ACEs (Narayan, 2017). BCEs are the antithesis of ACEs, experiences such as life stability, physical safety, and emotional care. Similarly, the positive impact that educators can have on students with ACEs is profound. For students with ACEs, a classroom teacher might be the most consistent, caring person in their world. Students can heal from ACEs when they are celebrated, comforted, listened to, asked for their opinions, exposed to new ideas, and treated with reliable kindness. Students with ACEs can thrive when they are in a supportive school environment, when teachers are creative, flexible, and patient when working with them, and when students get the resources they need (which often can go beyond the role of a teacher and into the role of a school counselor or mental health practitioner).

Helping students heal is a wonderful practice, yet it comes with its own hazards. Teachers are not only susceptible to having their own ACEs, but are susceptible to what is often called "second-hand trauma." Working with students who are dealing with difficult life circumstances takes a toll on educators. With that in mind, be the model of caring and consistency that your students need. But also remember to take care of yourself so that you can be the best for your students. This may include anything from timely breaks or hobbies on the weekend to finding the right level of professional help. Helping students with ACEs is tough work that can be frustrating, messy, and even hazardous. It's also profoundly important and rewarding. And ultimately, it's worth it.

Action Steps:

➢ **In light of the fact that so many of our students have had adverse childhood experiences, you are in a unique position to provide stability, consistency, and safety to students who have experienced trauma.**

➢ **Decide who is your most challenging student(s).**

➤ Next time they struggle, take an extra moment to consider what they may have been through (or go through each day), and respond appropriately, with grace and patience.

The Potential of Pictures

"It's a visual world and people respond to visuals." - Joe Sacco

"A photograph is usually looked at; seldom looked into." - Ansel Adams

If it's true that pictures paint a thousand words, why do teachers still try to use thousands of words to explain things to their students? Cue the "wamp wamp wamp" of Charlie Brown's teacher here. If you are not doing so already, stop talking occasionally, and show them some pictures! Pictures are not superficial. Pictures don't mean that they aren't reading or thinking deeply. On the contrary, the right pictures are out there to help teach content and increase depth of knowledge for student tasks. In the age of technology, your students are yearning to analyze, comment on, critique, enjoy, and critically think, talk, and write about images.

Granted, some courses cater to image use more than others. For example, High School U.S. History courses can refer to photographs of wars, the Great Depression, assassinations, and more. On the contrary, any topic prior to the early 1800s would have no photographs to analyze. But even when studying ancient civilizations, there are certainly photographs of artifacts, artwork, and structures that could be used. Teaching math concepts can take advantage of geometric shapes in the real world. For science, the possibilities are endless for using pictures related to physics, astronomy, biology, and more. Language arts should also be taking advantage of pictures as students are expected to analyze, predict, summarize, argue, and defend their positions. Any elective or enrichment course can do the same.

Using pictures can be powerful. For the sake of time, or because of a misguided attempt to help them learn, you might be tempted to break it all down and explain everything for your students. Remember, it is wonderful to model expert thinking for your learners, but don't forget to leave room for them to practice the analysis on some of the images as well. One of the easiest classroom activities is to encourage students to use context clues as they analyze an image. What is this? Where is this? Why do you think that? How do you know? Discuss with a neighbor. Students can even come up with their own questions. Comparing multiple images for similarities and differences can likewise allow for prolific discussion.

The gallery walk is another useful activity as students circulate the room to discuss what they see. Using images allows for successful classroom experiences for those to whom success does not come easily. Print copies if you must, project them on the walls, or share them in the digital classroom. Get images in front of your students and let them think.

Action Steps:

> ➤ Find an image to use as a lesson hook, learning segment, or lesson closure.
> ➤ List a series of questions that you can use to get students thinking about the image.
> ➤ Allow for students to ask their own questions.

Autonomy, Mastery, Purpose:
What Motivates Students?

*"Allow your passion to become your purpose, and it will
one day become your profession." - Gabriel Bernstein*

Conventional wisdom would suggest that workers are motivated by money, power, or recognition, but the research suggests otherwise. Certainly, for simple work tasks, monetary incentives work well. But for tasks that require cognitive skill or creativity, monetary incentives don't make a lick of difference. Best-selling author Daniel Pink has studied motivation in the workplace, and he boils motivation down to three main factors: autonomy, mastery, and purpose. These three factors are the key to productivity and fulfillment.

Autonomy refers to our professional and creative freedom. Instead of a manager saying, "Here is the incentive for completing a creative task," they should say, "you probably want to do something really cool, let me just get out of the way." Mastery refers to conquering something. It's why we like to get better at things. It's why we climb mountains, study languages, play sports, or learn songs on a guitar. Purpose refers to the greater significance of our work. We do it because it matters. We do it to improve things, to make a difference, or to make the world a better place. All three of these factors are highly motivating in and of themselves.

As working teachers, we know this to be anecdotally true. We don't want to be micromanaged by our supervisors. We are professionals who bring amazing effort and creativity to the table. Administrators may need to synchronize the opportunities, but then we prefer they get out of the way. We are also motivated by mastery. It is highly satisfying and motivating to improve our craft and become more effective classroom teachers. It is a wonderful feeling at the end of a school year when you know you and your students nailed it and had a fantastic year. We are motivated by purpose as well. The teaching profession is perhaps one of the easiest to connect to a larger purpose as we are shaping the youth, and by extension, shaping the future of the world.

Naturally, we ought to apply these truths to our students, who are similar in terms of what motivates them. If you want them to do amazing things, they aren't best incentivized by money, rewards, or good grades as much as by autonomy, mastery, and purpose. Carrots and sticks work for simple tasks such as establishing routines or managing behavior, but not for complicated tasks. The truth is, our students are going to perform better and find greater satisfaction the same way working adults do, through autonomy, mastery, and purpose.

Consider your next project. As you iron out the details, allow room for autonomy (e.g. selecting from a menu of topics), mastery (e.g. praising students for new skills), and purpose (e.g. explicit conversations about why their learning matters). The kids want to do something amazing anyway. As a teacher, you have the power to create opportunities for them to do just that.

Action Steps:

> **Regardless of grade level, have a discussion with your class about what motivates them.**

> **Ask them if they like to work autonomously, if they are intrinsically motivated by mastering a skill, and if they find purpose in what they are doing.**

> **Find ways to minimize your role and to position your students to practice autonomy, mastery, and purpose in the classroom.**

If You Haven't Already, Lose Your Cool Jacket

"There is something exciting about being in an environment in which it's really cool to be smart." - Freeman Hrabowski

"The mark of a true hero is humility." - Master Shifu (Kung Fu Panda)

My high school basketball coach used to refer to athletes with egos as having "cool jackets," meaning they walked around wearing arrogance that was so obvious, it was like an article of clothing you could see on them from miles away. He encouraged his players to lose their cool jackets on and off the court, and I have found this directly applicable to the classroom as well.

Whichever grade or subject you teach, kids benefit from connecting with their teachers. If you have a glaring haughtiness, your students are likely to pick up on it and will have a difficult time looking past it to connect with you. Let your students into your world, assuring them that you aren't too good for them. Show them your humility as well as your humanity.

One of the easiest ways to lose your cool jacket is to do something intentionally silly in front of your students. It not only entertains them, draws them in, and opens them up to learning, but it also humanizes you. I know teachers who sing to their students. Some performed cover songs for a mental break, some did lyric analysis lessons, and others did goofy, rhyming, pneumonic device ballads. I knew a P.E. teacher who had zero musical talent, but still sang to his students; they loved it. I have known teachers to dress up as Abe Lincoln, Dr. Seuss, or Albert Einstein, staying in character (with accent!) the entire day. I remember running up and down the aisles, screaming and high-fiving my students as we watched a clip of the 1982 Lake Placid Winter Olympics. The U.S. Hockey team beat the heavily favored Soviet team in what was dubbed the "Miracle on Ice." I'm not a huge hockey fan, and of course I already knew what was going to happen. But just as I expected, my ridiculousness puzzled them and captivated their attention so they latched on for the rest of the lesson.

A teacher's excitement is contagious; embrace that truth and take full advantage of it. Take the vulnerable step to do something outside of your comfort zone, something that may be silly. If you are still wearing one, take off your cool jacket for the sake of your student connections and for the sake of their learning.

Action Steps:

> ➤ **Reflect on whether you wear any cool jackets.**
> ➤ **Connect with students and connect them to their learning in new ways by being vulnerable, silly, excited, or doing something outside your comfort zone.**

Someone Is Thinking Critically:
Is It Your Students?

"I cannot teach anyone anything. I can only make them think." - Socrates

I once observed an 8th grade lesson in which the teacher showed an Electoral College map for the state of California. With the nation's highest population, California has many districts and he pointed out the clump of small districts near the Los Angeles and Bay Areas, contrasting them with the larger districts in the Sierra Nevada Range and northern reaches of the state. He explained that each district will always represent 1/538th of the national population and identified different areas of population density in the state. It was fascinating and the students were on the edge of their seats. Then he showed the Kansas version, Nevada version, and others, explaining all the same things. The kids grew more and more disinterested as they realized he was going to be doing the critical thinking for them. A golden opportunity to foster critical thinking was squandered.

Whether it is the confluence of causes and effects, solving multi-step computations, explaining how you came to an answer, or tackling a cross-curricular breakout box, teaching and learning is often about thinking critically. Sometimes, critical thinking is straightforward, and other times it is more nuanced and harder to get a finger on the critical-thinking pulse. Generally, teachers are much better at making connections and thinking critically than students. And with so much exciting content to cover, teachers, much like the well-intentioned teacher with the Electoral College lesson, will all-too-often do the critical thinking instead of letting their students do it.

It is an all-too familiar storyline: teacher talks, teacher explains, teacher makes connections, and students listen. In that storyline, critical thinking is optional, and students may or may not choose to mentally engage. Allow for intentional moments in each lesson where the students have opportunities to think critically. Of course, you (the teacher) are better at it and you may think you need to blast through content in order to get to that all-important unit or review lesson before state testing. However, going through all the content doesn't matter if you haven't let them think about it. If you don't have time to stop and let students think during your lessons, then some pacing adjustments are in order. Breadth may need to yield a bit to depth during the school year. After all, *much* content with no depth doesn't bode well, whereas *some* content where students think deeply will better prepare them to perform on assessments and in real life.

Action Steps:

> ➤ **Recall a recent lesson in which you did much of the talking or critical thinking.**

> ➤ **With the electoral college lesson as a model, what are some ways you could allow for your students to do the talking or critical thinking instead?**

Besides Knowledge and Skills, What Should You Teach?

"When teaching, light a fire, don't fill a bucket." - Dan Snow

When students leave your class at the end of the year, what should they take with them? A few facts? An understanding of concepts? A handful of ideas? Priceless skills? Yes, to all the above. It is a reasonable expectation to believe that they will take with them things like reading skills, content knowledge, the ability to analyze, think critically, form opinions, and enhance their academic abilities. But is there anything else?

Besides content knowledge and skills, I had a laundry list of other intangibles I wanted my students to take away with them. This included: showing respect for others, practicing kindness, demonstrating empathy, developing a curiosity for learning, having a sense of humor, appreciating the process, being comfortable with other perspectives, tolerating (even intolerant people), understanding laws of logic, knowing basic philosophical principles, comprehending rhetoric, and learning to persevere. My list went on and on.

I would presume that there are as many lists as there are teachers. Have you thought about the things you want to give your students that go beyond skills and knowledge? If you haven't, take a moment to jot down a few items that are important to you. Maybe your list goes in a syllabus, finds its way into a parent letter, or is laminated on the wall. Or maybe your list is private, informal, or pliable. In any case, you aren't a robot and you have so much to offer your students beyond the standard curriculum. Be ever mindful and deliberate about what else you teach your students.

Action Steps:

- ➤ Outside of content knowledge or academic skills, think about what you value and want your students to value.
- ➤ Make a list of some of these intangibles that you would like your students to take with them after being in your class.
- ➤ Consider things like character traits, attitude, or life skills.
- ➤ Decide whether it would be appropriate to share this list with your students, their parents, or both.

Being A Learning Leader
in The Classroom

"The central challenge for educational systems around the world is the substitution of effectiveness for popularity." - Douglas B. Reeves

Several years ago, Doug Reeves wrote a book called *The Learning Leader*, which looked at student achievement progress in one of four categories: losing, lucky, learning, leading (Reeves, 2010). The variables are whether students are improving, and whether you know why. Using his model, a school is either losing (students not improving and you don't know why), lucky (students improving and you don't know why), learning (students not improving yet you know why), or leading (students improving and you know why).

Although Reeves wrote with school and district leaders in mind, his model should be applied to every classroom by every teacher. Before I knew better, I gave students an assessment and wondered how they would perform. Sometimes they nailed it; sometimes not. I often over-analyzed my instruction, dwelling on what I could have done better. I really didn't like being behind the eight-ball. Over time as I improved my craft, I recognized that there were practical approaches that wouldn't leave me wondering how my students would fare on assessments. These approaches included frequent checks for understanding, using whiteboards, informal assessments, surveying the room, pre-tests (or group pre-tests), and teacher modeling.

If you want to measure student growth from the start of a unit, track reading proficiency from August, or measure changes from the previous school year on testing, try implementing strategies that will show you how they will perform before they are actually called on to do so. In this way, you can have peace of mind. It means that when students improve, you'll know exactly why. It means you won't be losing or lucky. You'll be a learning leader in your classroom.

Action Steps:

- ➤ **Ask yourself the following questions:**
- ➤ **Do you know if your students are improving?**
- ➤ **Can you explain why?**
- ➤ **Are you losing, lucky, learning, or leading?**

Know Your Teaching Standards

"The quality of an exemplary teacher is demonstrated by their willingness to set and maintain the highest standards for themselves and their students." - Robert John Meehan

Teachers are held to the highest of standards. Whether we are talking about the NBPTS (National Board for Professional Teaching Standards), individual state teaching standards, the Danielson framework, district-specific induction standards, Stronge's TEPES (Teacher Effectiveness Performance Evaluation System), or the INTASC standards (Interstate New Teacher Assessment and Support Consortium), there are plenty of guidelines in place to measure and evaluate teachers. For the most part, each of these sets of standards focus on similar aspects of the job. Central components tend to include things like supporting students, managing the learning environment, building curriculum, delivering instruction, overseeing assessments, and upholding levels of professionalism.

These standards are not on par with the Holy Scriptures. They are not enshrined like the Magna Carta. Nor are they living, breathing documents like the U.S. Constitution. But make no mistake, they are written on purpose. They are in place to maintain a standard of excellence for our profession, and ultimately to help students. Consider the following three challenges as you consider the standards by which you are evaluated:

First, get to know your teaching standards better. Be able to identify the larger categories of standards, as well as specific standards therein. Take some time to see the forest for the trees, considering how they work together to address the work of the teacher in support of student learning. I have known some districts to make trifolds for each substandard, complete with rationale, explanations, and recommended strategies. Know your standards and know why they exist.

Second, achieve mastery of your standards. It is one thing to reference the standards or have familiarity with them. It is quite another to truly master them in your daily undertakings. It may already be prescribed by your district to select goals or objectives, but if not, set measurable professional goals on your own. Select new standards each year on which you aspire to improve. This practice will be worth the time, both for you and for your students.

Third, share your wisdom with respect to mastering the teaching standards. After all, teaching is best practiced in collaboration with others. Sometimes, fellow teachers need extra support. Encourage your colleagues as they strive to master the teaching standards and improve their craft as well.

Action Steps:

> ➢ Read through your teaching standards, seeking to better understand why they exist and why they are written the way they are.

> ➢ With a growth mindset and using your teaching standards, identify aspects of your craft that you could work to improve.

> ➢ Share what you are doing with a colleague, specifically how you have grown, are growing, or plan to grow.

Contrary to Popular Belief,
Film Is Good for Learning

"The screen is a magic medium. It has such power that it can retain interest as it conveys emotions and moods that no other art form can hope to tackle." - Stanley Kubrick

I loved showing movies in class at opportune times during the school year. Some teachers think movies and rigor go together like water and oil. I agree that showing movies in the classroom can be a colossal waste of time. If you are showing movies all year, you had better be teaching a film class. Yet with the right approach, movies can also be tremendous learning tools used by highly effective teachers.

Movies have been part of pop culture for over a century and are "popular" by definition. Integrating movies into the curriculum is a worthwhile pursuit that can be accomplished without having to show entire films or burn through swaths of instructional time. A word of caution before we go further: not all students come from the same cultural backgrounds. As teachers, we cannot assume that all our students have the same frame of reference when it comes to popular movies. "You know, like when Scar kills Mufasa in *The Lion King*" can strike an emotional chord with some learners, but doesn't mean a thing to others. Whether or not students have prior knowledge of the films and references you make, you can still use movies to peak student interest, draw them into your lessons, and converge seamlessly with curriculum.

While teaching high school history, I realized there were dozens of World War II films that would have been a joy to watch with students. That was an unrealistic goal with respect to instructional time, so instead of showing any of these films in class, I combined three other approaches, all of which worked to maintain a high level of rigor for my students. The following suggestions are specific to a unit on World War II but can be universally applied as well.

First, present contextualized, digestible five to ten-minute scenes, combined with other critical thinking activities to deepen the complexity of a lesson. For example, take the 2001 HBO series *Band of Brothers*. The entire mini-series is profoundly powerful, but I hardly had two weeks to cover the unit, and I couldn't dedicate the whole two weeks to watching one television show. Instead, I chose to spend a few minutes giving my students context before showing them the paratrooper jump scene. Meanwhile, my students were tasked with identifying locations on a map of Europe, digesting primary sources, and placing notes on graphic organizers. The paratrooper scene brought the subject to life, coaxing them to dive into the rest of the material with a newfound fervor.

Second, expose students to selected movie trailers. For the World War II unit, I used topical trailers such as *Schindler's List* or *The Pianist* during our Holocaust lesson, or *Bridge on the River Kwai* before studying the Pacific Theater. Admittedly, I did this with compound intentions. For one, critical thinking was promoted by asking my students to predict, connect, and question specific elements within the trailer. Additionally, the viewing was used as a hook for the lesson. The trailer would build interest around the historical topic. And by showing the trailer, I was encouraging them to go watch the film at home as well (and many did). After all, a trailer is nothing more than a commercial for the film.

Third, create a "films to watch" list for each unit, trimester, grading period, etc. Your students can then engage with several fantastic films on their own time, which easily link to their studies. For me, *Gandhi, Saving Private Ryan, Dr. Strangelove, Hotel Rwanda* were big hits. It was a guileful way to introduce something of a flipped classroom model. Many students watched movies before our lessons on related topics, bringing with them background knowledge, and tremendously enhancing the conversations in the room.

Movies are made to tell stories and often relate to history and English classes. However, the same strategies can be used in math with short clips from *Good Will Hunting, A Beautiful Mind,* or *Stand and Deliver,* for example. Science classes can incorporate clips from *Bill Nye, Magic School Bus, October Sky, Apollo 13,* or *Jurassic Park.* Clips from YouTube educators such as "The Backyard Scientist" and "How Ridiculous" can have a similar impact on lesson suspense.

Action Steps:

> ➢ Whatever you teach, consider how you could take advantage of the popularity of movies and clips to hook, engage, and prime students for your lessons.

Inquiry Vs. Direct Instruction:
Is There A Balance?

"Before I came here, I was confused about this subject. Having listened to your lecture I am still confused, but on a higher level." - Enrico Fermi

Across content areas, there is a recent movement away from direct instruction and toward inquiry-based lessons (there were similar movements in the 1960s and 1980s). This includes ideas such as: emphasis on primary source document analysis in social studies, a move to next generation science standards in science, established group roles in CPM mathematics, and the shift to more non-fiction reading in language arts. I have known teachers to embrace this and known others to resist it. The truth is, both sides had valid reasons for doing so. The embracers of inquiry-based lessons point out that students learn more, retain more, and come alive with a self-discovery approach to learning. The resisters point out that allowing students to discover takes much longer, leads to frustrating learning experiences, and usually means they will never get through the curriculum.

Of course, there is a healthy equilibrium between the two approaches. One of the best lessons I have ever seen came from a math teacher who switched back and forth between direct instruction and student-inquiry during her pre-algebra lesson. There was hardly a wasted second of instructional time and the teacher provided support and direction at the most opportune moments. She used huddle groups, a variety of check-for-understanding strategies to redirect when needed. She used the phrase "red light" to call attention and drive direction, and "green light" to release students back to work. The best way to describe it was that she facilitated while the students dug in. I witnessed authentic light-bulb moments as students figured it out without the teacher spelling it out.

Your direct instruction lessons don't have to be like watching paint dry; lackluster and uninspiring. Allow for your students to have the freedom to think and solve problems on their own. Your inquiry-based lessons don't have to feel frenzied or confused either. Stop to give your students timely direction. There are times where it is best to let your students struggle through the process and figure it out, and there are times when it is best to instruct and offer guidance.

Action Steps:

> ➢ **You serve students with different needs and learning preferences that can change as circumstances warrant.**
> ➢ **Each day be mindful of striking the right balance between inquiry and instruction in your lessons.**

Involve Students in Their Learning

"Truly wonderful the mind of a child is." - Yoda

"I loved learning; it was school I hated. I used to cut school to go learn something." - Eric Jensen

Benjamin Franklin famously said, "Tell me and I forget, teach me and I may remember, involve me and I learn." Franklin was a Renaissance man of the late-Enlightenment and of the American Revolution, He was on to something with this line of thinking. For teachers, his saying suggests that lecture isn't sufficient, that explaining is better, and that active learning is best. Scholarly research supports Franklin's assertions. In K-12, active learning is effective across disciplines (Eison & Bonwell, 1993), generates excitement (Bonwell & Eison, 1991), promotes autonomy (Fredricks, 2014), curbs disengagement (Reeve, Jang, Carrell, Jeon & Barch, 2004), and is found to be effective in higher education as well (Konings, 2010). And if we consider our own classes, we know this to be anecdotally true.

There are plenty of strategies out there that involve students. For instance, GLAD Strategies (Guided Language Acquisition Design) aim to ensure that all students read, write, and access grade level content by promoting the use of academic language, drawing pictures, retelling, and graphic organizers. Other teachers establish systems of structured-student interaction, facilitate hands-on-experiments, or lead Socratic seminars and inquiry lessons, facilitate role-playing, comic strips, or offer students choices in their learning.

A great lecturer in the K-12 classroom is well-intentioned, but misguided. No matter how entertaining you think you are, no matter how great a speaker you might be, no matter how good you are at explaining things, stop talking and involve your students. You will become a better teacher, your students will better retain information, and you will all have more fun. Involving your students is a win-win-win situation.

Action Steps:

> ➤ **You have told your students plenty and taught them a great deal. What is a fresh approach you might take to *involve* them in their learning?**

Everything Is Beowulf, You Know

"We are all storytellers. We all live in a network of stories. There isn't a stronger connection between people than storytelling." - Jimmy Neil Smith

Kids are hard-wired for stories, a truth of which I took full advantage in the classroom. For instance, I often facilitated a compare/contrast between familiar Disney stories and the history we studied. *The Lion King* borrows from the Epic of Sundiata, *Aladdin* incorporates elements of Muhammad's life, *Emperor's New Groove* is set in the Incan South America, and so on. There were many others as well, but then there was Beowulf. No other story was referenced with such frequency. *Beowulf* topped the list.

When you teach English Language Arts or related content, you'd better know about *Beowulf*. This 10th century Danish epic poem contains most of the archetypal characters and plot elements that have been used in stories since. Only a few other stories can claim that (Homer, Virgil, Ovid, and the writers of Gilgamesh, Mahabharata, and Ramayana also have strong cases). So, why am I bringing this up? Because there are two very different, but very important points to make here for the classroom teacher.

First, literally use *Beowulf* in your classroom. I spend a good portion of an ELA summer school class comparing *Beowulf* to *The Hobbit* and *Lord of the Rings*. Tolkien taught on *Beowulf* at Oxford, after all. Check this out: Unferth is Grema Wormtongue, Hrothgar is King Théoden, Beowulf is Frodo, etc. I facilitated as my students discovered the associations and it was priceless. The extent to which you expose your students to the story will depend on grade level and ability, but all students can relate to stories. They want to discuss and analyze stories as well. Critical thinking is a universal skill in educational standards across states and grade levels. With that in mind, find a way to compare Unferth, Hrothgar, Beowulf, Breca, or Grendel to characters in other stories you expose your classes to.

Second, don't reinvent the wheel. You can be a highly effective rock-star-of-a-teacher without having to come up with a secret formula or a magical set of lessons. There have been many rock-star teachers before you and ones that currently work around you, so just figure out what they did and what they are doing that works so well. Since teaching is one of the oldest professions in the world, there is a wealth of knowledge from which to draw. Just as stories across the centuries tend to use the same archetypal characters and plot elements, find some things that work in the classroom and stick with them. *Beowulf*, baby. Apply it.

Action Steps:

> ➢ **Capitalize on the fact that many have come before you and have done what you do with great success. Don't reinvent the wheel. Also, capitalize on our students' love of stories.**

> ➢ **With your guidance, allow them to think critically by comparing stories, characters, or other content specific concepts.**

What They Remember 27 Years Later

"They may forget what you said but they will never
forget how you made them feel." - Carl Buechner

"Hey, you were my teacher 27 years ago and I remember everything about your class. I regularly refer back to each of the hundreds of lessons you taught me," said no former student ever. No matter how wonderful you are, after students leave your class in the spring, they won't remember as much as you hope. This sober truth has a number of implications.

First, don't take yourself too seriously. Elementary teachers tend to figure this out sooner than most. Some high school teachers never quite figure it out. Sure, you're probably a wonderful teacher, but don't get so worked up if your students make mistakes, act up, forget things, or treat your lessons as if they are anything other than the pure gold that you may believe they are. They are human and so are you. Lighten up and let yourself laugh a little.

Second, they will remember certain lessons, and determining which lessons become the memorable ones is up to you. Is it the mind-blowing science experiment? The themed historical dress-day? Using M&Ms for arithmetic? A novel that knocks their socks off or touches their hearts? I knew a group of teachers that aimed to have at least one "memorable" lesson for each unit. They did a pretty good job of it and students talked about those learning events years later.

Third, there is the matter of legacy. You still have a chance to make a lasting impact on your students in all sorts of other ways. What will be your legacy? Students tend to remember their teachers in absolutes; nice or mean, easy or hard, funny or stoic, engaging or boring, etc. In addition to these labels, they will also likely remember how they felt in your class. What will they say about how you treated them? Did you pay attention to them? Did they feel supported? Encouraged? Ridiculed? Embarrassed? Challenged? Cared for?

It is a strong likelihood that some of your students will remember you in 27 years. How you approach your students will have a profound impact on what they remember and how they remember you. Make learning fun. Show them you care. Take an interest in their academic successes. There is no good reason why you should not strive every day to shape a positive legacy with your students. Challenge yourself this week to make a memorable learning experience for your students. Truth be told, most of us became teachers at least in part because of teachers that inspired us when we were students. And you are bound to have some future educators in your classes, so set a good example.

Action Steps:

➢ **Consider your legacy as an educator.**

➢ **How many students do you have in your classroom each year? How many years are you likely to work?**

➢ **Use simple multiplication to determine how many students will you have in your classroom over the course of your career. Write down what you want students to remember about you and your class 27 years from now.**

➢ **Then ask yourself what you may need to change in order to make this a reality.**

I Talk, You Listen, No One Learns

"Never miss a good chance to shut up." - Will Rogers

"Cool story, bro." - indifferent, insolent juvenile from the 2010s

When a presenter at a professional development session suggested that I hand notes to the students instead of lecturing and expecting them to take notes, I thought they were nuts. Up to that point, I figured that student notetaking was at the heart of teaching and learning in middle or high school. To suggest that I simply omit that step seemed ridiculous. "What else is there to do?" I thought to myself. With greater contemplation, I began to see the genius behind this suggestion.

First, consider the traditional lecture approach. Lecture with student notetaking requires little critical thinking. High schools are ripe with it. Middle schools can have their share of it. I've even seen it in first grade classrooms. "Copying like a monkey" is what a former principal used to call it. Monkey-copying doesn't enhance critical thinking, it inhibits critical thinking. Lecture-based lessons make critical thinking optional at best and non-existent at worst. The teacher is thinking critically and inviting students to follow along with little or no accountability or higher-order thinking. Some students can still learn this way, but for the vast majority it is brutal and largely ineffective.

Providing students with guided notes or structured fill-in-the-blanks is a step in the right direction, but still missing the point. Handing out follow-along-notes is just an excuse to continue lecturing. Although it seemed counterintuitive to me at first (certainly different from how I was trained to teach), there was a far better option. I realized that I could facilitate any number of activities that required higher-level thinking if I simply provided the bulk of the notes or information for my students first.

For me, it required a serious paradigm shift since I was so used to students taking notes. Here is a tangible example. First, provide students with the definitions to your list of vocabulary words (saving 20 minutes of instructional time). Then do something better with it. Have them create visuals for each word instead. Have them write a poem using 7 of the 15 the words instead. Have them incorporate half of the words as they create three multiple-choice questions instead. Have them create a storyboard using at least ten of the words instead. Students by and large want to do creative things. Design lessons accordingly. Your students will be more than happy to stop copying like monkeys and oblige.

Action Steps:

> ➢ **When do you anticipate students will take notes? Next time, shake things up and give them the notes instead, and with the instructional time that you save, ask them to do a creative or higher-order thinking task with the information.**

Religion and Politics Without Leading to Trouble

"Along with two thieves, he was executed by the authorities about two thousand years ago. Yet today, from countless paintings, statues, and buildings, from literature and history, from personality and institution, from profanity, popular song, and entertainment media, from confession and controversy, from legend and ritual - Jesus stands quietly at the center of the contemporary world, as he himself predicted. He so graced the ugly instrument on which he died that the cross has become the most widely exhibited and recognized symbol on earth." - Dallas Willard (USC Professor of Philosophy)

My first department was a high-functioning, tight-knit group of misfits, and we were about as religiously diverse as could be. I was the token Christian, alongside an agnostic, a practicing Jew, a Catholic-Buddhist, an atheist, and a skeptic. Some were Democrat, some Republican, and some neither. One was both. From our varying backgrounds, we had a handful of key commonalities. First, we all taught religious and political content, as was prescribed by state history standards. Second, we maintained professionalism with each other, showing respect, listening actively, and playing fair. Third, we never found trouble with students, parents, or administrators on our handling of the inevitable religious or political discussions that emerged in our middle school history classrooms.

Most state standards address religious and political topics in almost all grade levels. Ancient and medieval history covers major world religions. High school history and government classes face politics head on. And even if you don't teach directly on the topic, Dallas Willard's quote reminds us that Jesus tends to come up sooner or later.

Our department of misfits was a model on this issue, sticking to facts when teaching about Buddhism, Taoism, Islam, Shinto, or Judaism.

Christianity came up in many units (Rome, Renaissance, Reformation, Exploration, etc.). We focused on history, allowing students to reach their own conclusions about beliefs. It was exciting, and even for the others who weren't Christians, they couldn't deny the impact of Jesus on our world today and felt a duty or obligation to get the history right when they taught. Some events from history shine a bad light on those that claim to be Christians (the Medici papacy, the Inquisition, Columbus, Da Gama, Henry VIII) and some events are compellingly persuasive (historical evidence for the validity of the gospels, for instance). When things got dicey or when students asked tough questions, some go-to teacher lines included things like, "Yes, some people believe that and some don't" or "I'm not in a place to tell you what you should or shouldn't believe" or "That's a great question. You should talk to your parents about that one." In much the same way, confronting political issues is often inevitable. Using phrases like, "well, a conservative or liberal might say this because..." or "a commonly used counter-argument to consider would be..." help to keep the learning process dynamic without inputting bias.

Tough topics like religious or political discussion in the classroom can and should be addressed without stirring up controversy. Yes, it includes teaching historical facts and sticking to the standards. It also should include a big dose of professionalism, respect, listening, and prudence.

Action Steps:

> **Think about where religious discussions arise during the school year.**

> **How might you work to keep the learning process dynamic without inputting bias or stirring up unnecessary controversy?**

The Top Ten List: A Gateway
to Critical Thinking

"Lists are to the reader's eye what Brad Pitt is to the paparazzi. You just can't get enough." - Kara Pernice

My wife and I recently planned an anniversary trip to Spain. We picked up a travel guide with information about the cities. The guide listed most topics by way of "Top Ten Lists," including best places to eat, most popular museums, great places to get a coffee, and so on. I couldn't put the thing down. It spoke to my inner desire to sort and rank. Similarly, I can't get enough of top 100 lists, such as *Rolling Stone Magazine*'s top 100 musicians, or American Film Institute's top 100 films.

I recognize that my fascination with lists stems from a desire to learn and organize information. More importantly, I recognize that students have similar desires. Not only do I make a point to rank things as I teach, I leave room for students to predict, rank, and scrutinize lists as well. Ten is common, but of course you can have lists of three, eleven, or twenty-two, or any other number. Sometimes lists matters of fact, such as deadliest battles of the Civil War, longest words, largest integers, richest people, or best-selling books.

Top ten lists can also be very subjective. And even when they are subjective, you can ask your students to use higher-level critical thinking as they justify their rankings. Greatest scientists. Most important founding fathers. Most devious Disney villains. Hardest words to spell. Top ten math concepts from this course. Most influential novels of the 20th century. Best Dr. Seuss books. The applications are endless.

Use lists to organize content. Use them as pneumonic devices as students recall information. Ask students to use objective top ten lists to organize material. Use subjective top ten lists to support critical thinking and ask them to defend ranking decisions. Use lists over and over. Take advantage of student tendencies to sort and organize. The lists that students generate are important, but not as important as the conversations and critical thinking processes along the way.

Action Steps:

> ➤ **Plan to incorporate a list in an upcoming lesson, allowing students to predict, rank, or scrutinize.**

Decorating Your Room on Purpose

"A room should never allow the eye to settle in one place. It should smile at you and create fantasy." - Juan Montoya

Sometimes, classrooms are so organized it is disturbing. And sometimes, they are so bare or in such disarray, I don't know how the students can tolerate it. Whether your room is a work of art, severely lacking, hoarder-status, or somewhere in between, the way your room is decorated speaks volumes. Whether you mean to or not, your room says much about your pedagogical style, your work ethic, your purpose, what you value, and what intentions you have for your students.

A lack of purposed décor doesn't do much. It doesn't galvanize students, showcase their work, establish routines, or incite thoughts about content or the learning process. Your room doesn't need to perpetually show off fresh, Pinterest-ready student work. It doesn't need to be featured in a magazine. But it should serve a purpose, even multiple purposes. I've known teachers to effectively design island-themed rooms or use stringed lights to establish a relaxed mood. I've seen minimalist rooms that were more helpful for students than cluttered ones. My high school English teacher had nothing on the walls, save for a Jim Morrison poster that referenced themes we studied in the class; freedom, personal expression, rebellion.

When I first organized my own classroom, I laminated and hung up several maps that I had pulled out of a hand-me-down collection of National Geographic magazines. I asked myself, "When students daydream or need a brain break, what do I want them to look at?" The use of maps was my answer. For one student who habitually stared at the ceiling, I even put a map above her seat; with jocularity, of course. I later outfitted my room with giant wall-to-wall world maps, one for each side of the classroom.

One colleague snaked a historical timeline around the walls near the ceiling. Another featured a massive periodic table. Others blew up covers of famous novels, framed inspirational quotes, or posted humorous memes about classroom rules. Many teachers showcase the best student work. Some showcase all student work, no matter how wonderful or dreadful. These ideas and countless others have their places in our classrooms. Take a moment to consider why you decorate your room the way you do. Your four walls can do much more than just hold up the roof. Your four walls can display, teach, entertain, inspire, and speak volumes.

Action Steps:

> ➢ **Ask yourself (or if you are so bold, ask someone you trust) the following questions to evaluate your room décor:**
> ➢ **When it comes to my room décor, what am I saying without saying it?**
> ➢ **What values am I communicating about my values?**
> ➢ **How does this help my students to learn?**

Ifs, Ands...No Buts:
The Power of Positivity

*"Being positive isn't pretending that everything is good,
it's seeing the good in everything." - Unknown*

Kids are often wrong. It's part of learning. Most are wrong some of the time. Some are wrong most of the time. A few are wrong just about all the time. When they are wrong in their reasoning, in their approach, in their responses, or in their conclusions, what you say next matters greatly. This is especially true with reluctant learners. Even if you are naturally kind or encouraging, too many "buts" can take a harmful psychological toll on a young mind, making the child feel like they never quite get the answer correct.

Next time one of your students says something completely wrong, take a mental note about how you respond. Do you default to some form of "no"? Do you correct them with a "but" or a "however"? I'm not talking about off-task behavior where the teacher clearly needs to intervene with firm correction. I'm talking about when teaching and learning is flowing or when students are being vulnerable. When a student offers a genuine attempt, "no" is the last thing you should use to answer. Correcting them with "but" can also be dispiriting. Possible teacher responses to a student that is clearly off-base might include:

- "Interesting. That's what I thought at first, too."
- "I can tell you gave that some thought."
- "That's a great start, who can add to that?"
- "Nice. Can you walk me through your thinking?"
- "Do you know about this other viewpoint?"

One of my favorite practices in the classroom was not to validate student responses at all. I would consecutively call on at least half a dozen students with the same question, giving no indication whether any of them were right or wrong. Sometimes students incorrectly assumed the first answer was wrong since I continued to call on others. Sometimes I was digging for more. It kept them on their toes and maintained a healthy anxiety in the classroom. Eventually when I addressed the responses, I still made a point to affirm my students.

Even if only for one learning segment at a time, challenge yourself to be aware of how you respond to student answers that may not be on the right track. The way you foster confidence and growth can have lasting impacts on young minds. After all, words are powerful. The words of a teacher particularly so.

Action Steps:

➢ **Pay attention to a lesson in which you interact with students (or audio record if needed).**

➢ **Determine how you respond to students who may not be on the right track.**

➢ **Do you rebuke them, judge them, or correct them?**

➢ **Do you redirect, encourage, or praise them?**

➢ **Do you use "if" and "and" or do you overuse "no" or "but" or "however"?**

The WIIFM: What's in It for Me?

"When the why is clear, the how is easy." - Unknown

A common teacher fallacy is to assume that students place the same value on learning that teachers do. Your students might be compliant, but that doesn't mean they are intrinsically motivated or that they care a lick about your lesson. Envision yourself in a student desk during a future lesson and ask yourself, "What's in it for me?" If your aim is for students to care, the answer to the WIIFM question has to be more than: *I'll get a good grade, I'll get to go to recess on time, my mom won't be mad at me,* or *I can go home when the bell rings.* For the average student in school, the answer to WIIFM might be "not much." As teachers, we can do better for our learners.

The good news is that there are ways to make sure your students know why they are doing what they are doing, and to ensure they have a decent answer to the WIIFM question. Here are a few ideas.

- Have an intentional discussion about how the knowledge will impact them in the future.

- List the variety of professions that use skills like the ones you are using in the classroom.

- Emphasize that they will build on this in subsequent lessons, later units, future grade levels, and with greater complexity.

If students know what they are learning and why it matters, they have a clearer, more holistic view of their learning experience, something education leaders refer to as "visible learning."

In my experience, one of the best ways to answer the WIIFM is to relate the content to student experiences. This can be done with any and all types of content. Are you teaching Social Studies? History is full of stories involving friends, families, power struggles, disagreements, betrayal, redemption, and many other themes that students can relate to. Reading and literature have similar links with these themes as well. Science is almost too easy. The scientific method can intersect learning with just about anything from household items to chemical reactions to *"Wow! I've always wondered how that worked."* Math teachers know that math is found everywhere. I've known some math teachers to send students on school-wide scavenger hunts to scope out various shapes and other mathematical concepts in real life.

Before you plan your next lesson, put yourself in your students' shoes and ask some questions. "What's in it for me?" "What do you want?" "What motivates you?" "What's in it for *you*?" Help them through their thoughts and make sure they have a decent answer.

Action Steps:

➢ **Envision yourself in a student desk during a future lesson and ask yourself, "What's in it for me?" If your aim is for students to care, the answer should go beyond compliance or grades.**

Primacy-Recency Principle:
Start Strong, End Strong

"I suffer from short term memory loss. It runs in my family. At least I think it does. Where are they?" - Dory

At a professional development, I was presented with ten sets of three-letter sequences and then asked to memorize them in 30 seconds. Most teachers in the room memorized 3 or 4, some as many as 6 or 7. Interestingly, almost everyone tended to remember the first few sequences, or the last few. The middle sequences were largely forgotten. The point being made was that of the primacy-recency principle, which states that people tend to memorize that which they hear first and that which they hear last better than everything in between. There are many practical applications to primacy-recency in the classroom.

First, the early moments of a learning segment are priceless. This is the time when students are most likely to be focused and attentive. If you take the first ten minutes of class checking homework completion, going over last night's math problems, taking role, or having students copy down the new set of spelling words, you are not exploiting the primacy-recency principle. Apart from a well-placed hook, it's best to get right into the lesson by introducing the main idea and learning objective. This way, students have clarity about what they are setting out to accomplish together.

Second, unless you do it for a specific learning purpose, avoid asking a shot-in-the-dark question like, "What do you think antidisestablishmentarianism means?" or "Who thinks they know what this concept is all about?" When the first several answers are inevitably silly, wrong, or both, some students will remember the incorrect answers, which were spoken first instead of the correct answers, which were revealed afterward.

Third, it is crucial to take lesson closure seriously. If you end with some variation of a learning objective recap, you're on the right track. If you end with fluff to fill time, such as, "That's the end of the lesson, go ahead and pack up a little early," or "So, what is everyone doing this weekend?" you're missing an invaluable piece of the learning process. Since the primacy-recency principle suggests that they are more likely to remember lesson opening and lesson closure, capitalize on this at the beginning and ending of each learning segment.

Action Steps:

> ➢ **Examine the approximate length of your lesson plan.**
> ➢ **Take care that the main idea is addressed early, when students are paying attention.**
> ➢ **Make sure you revisit this main idea during closure as well.**

Have You Thought Through Homework Philosophies?

"I leave homework to the last minute because I will be older and therefore wiser." - Unknown

Homework, of course, is schoolwork done at home or outside of school. There are at least two types of thinking on the subject. Both are at opposite ends of a spectrum and make valid points. Your own personal view may be a blend of the two, or something entirely different. What matters is that you have given some thought to your homework philosophy. It would be a shame if a teacher went an entire career burdening their students with homework without ever really thinking about why they assign homework in the first place. It would be equally unfortunate if a teacher never assigned homework when a certain approach to homework might have benefited their students.

Consider these two opposing views on homework before formulating or calibrating your own homework philosophy:

- On one end of the spectrum, some educators see homework as an essential part of the learning process. From this perspective, the benefits of homework are numerous. To start, teachers can take advantage of extended learning opportunities outside of the instructional day. Assuming gradual release and checking for understanding has occurred in class first, students have an opportunity to work independently while at home. Or perhaps you practice a flipped classroom and students are exposed to the material at home, meaning they are ready to come engage with the material at school. Either way, homework is a capacity-building exercise as students are given a clear responsibility. Just as with a real job with deadlines, they must rise to the occasion, or face the consequences.

- On the other end of the spectrum, some educators see homework as completely unnecessary, and even harmful. I came across a teacher meme that turned it into an acronym: "h.o.m.e.w.o.r.k. is half-of-my-energy-wasted-on-random-knowledge." These teachers don't trust students to do the work at home or to do it right. They would rather control the work process in the classroom. From this perspective, teachers also don't want to waste valuable instructional time on homework checks and corrections. Teachers end up spinning their wheels as they work to hold students accountable for doing homework instead of focusing on teaching. Homework has also been disputed on the basis that students could better spend their free time with extracurricular activities, resting, or bonding with family.

Is your homework load appropriate for your grade level or content area? According to board policy in many districts, homework usually increases in higher grade levels.

Action Steps:

> Whether or not to assign it is just one of many considerations when it comes to homework. Besides formulating your overall philosophy on the topic, consider how you would answer the following questions as you think through or solidify your perspective. Be an active listener as these discussions take place in your circles.

> Could you reasonably explain your homework perspective to your students, parents, colleagues, or administrators?

> Is your grading of homework unnecessarily complicated, weighted, or sucking up instructional time?

> Are you ultimately teaching content or responsibility by the way you address homework?

> Do you flip and do you know why you flip?

> Does a flipped classroom model sway your opinion on the necessity of homework?

The Educational Conservationist

"Si fractum non sit, noli id reficere."

The adage "If it ain't broke, don't fix it" was penned by Bert Lance in 1977 and is used in proper context all the time, but it is also a go-to phrase for many teachers who are too lazy or too reluctant to change. On the flip side, some teachers are so quick to jump on the latest bandwagons, you'd swear they were swayed by whomever they talked to last. The good news is that there is a third option. Let me introduce you to the *educational conservationist*.

The educational conservationist is not just a progressive looking to abandon past practices and find the next great thing in education. Nor are they simply a traditionalist that sticks with tried-and-true approaches in the classroom without giving new ideas a shot. Instead, the educational conservationist is the best of both worlds, hanging on to and scrutinizing that which works, while looking for new ideas to debut and add to their repertoire. Our young scholars are ever-changing, as we should be. Educational trends come and go, and they will continue to do so long as there are children to be taught. Using your professional discernment, stick with what works, but keep your mind open to new ideas as well.

The approach of the educational conservationist is nothing new. It's the same formula found all over the social sciences. In fact, it's exactly what has happened in the progression of Western Philosophy over the last two thousand years--according to G.W.F. Hegel, anyway. It's like this: An idea sprouts. An opposing idea arises to challenge. A blending of the two occurs. Thesis—antithesis—synthesis.

Using this same approach with the leading ideas in education will be similarly useful as you navigate the endless schools-of-thought that will emerge throughout your career. You can be grounded and mobile at the same time. In fact, as a teacher you must be.

Action Steps:

➢ Think about which label best describes you as an educator: progressive, traditionalist, or educational conservationist.

➢ If you tend to be progressive, consider proven practices that have their merits, have withstood the test of time, and continue to be effective.

➢ If you are a traditionalist, consider new ideas that could enhance the teaching and learning in your classroom.

➢ If you are an educational conservationist, perpetually examine what you bring in and what you discard as you improve your craft.

Love Your Content; Love Your Pupils

"Love the Lord with all your heart and with all your soul and with all your strength. These commandments that I give you today are to be on your hearts. Impress them on your children. Talk about them when you sit at home and when you walk along the road, when you lie down and when you get up." - Deuteronomy 6:5-7

Moses was onto something when he wrote these words to the Hebrews some 3,800 year ago. It was said that ancient Hebrew children heard every line of the scriptures, including these ones, from the mouths of their fathers before reaching adulthood. Regardless of your exposure to Judeo-Christian teaching, Moses offers universal advice to teachers. In fact, it's advice that could make or break your teaching career.

For teachers, the advice is to love your content and love your children. The students might not be your children in the biological sense that Moses proposed, and classroom teachers should recognize this distinction and maintain healthy boundaries. However, teachers are role models who have been entrusted with rooms full of impressionable minds. In fact, most governments use "in loco parentis," meaning "in place of a parent," as a legal term to describe the responsibility placed upon schools to take care of children.

Moses is saying that when you are teaching something of value it ought to be on your hearts (love what you teach), and you should impress them on your children (teach it to those whom you love). Love your content and love your pupils. Some teachers love their subject, some teachers love the kids, some love both, and some love neither. A teacher who loves neither is in the wrong line of work. A teacher who loves just one or the other is setting themselves up for many years of unfulfilling work and resentment. A teacher who loves both is on track for a fruitful and satisfying career. Take a page from Moses. Love your content and love your pupils.

Action Steps:

➤ Resolve that each day you will find purpose in choosing to love your content and love your pupils.

➤ On days when you are down, remind yourself of this resolution and purpose

Become A Master, Go Back to School

"Intelligence without ambition is a bird without wings." - Dali

From a certain perspective, college degrees are overrated. Plenty of entrepreneurs have made their fortunes without traditional higher education. From their garages, Gates built Microsoft and Jobs built Apple. LeBron and Kobe went straight from high school to the NBA. Ellen DeGeneres and John D. Rockefeller didn't go to college either. These folks were wicked smart and hugely successful. I'm sure you can think of a few "uneducated" people in your life who are also quite intelligent or successful. And on the flip side, I'm sure you can also think of people who have useless or overpriced degrees.

No matter how many exceptions you think of, they are still exceptions. In most cases, higher education is a valuable pursuit. It keeps you sharp and leads to more opportunities and higher salaries. This is especially true of educators. In many countries, classroom teachers are required to have a degree and credential before being hired. Salary schedules often encourage teachers to pursue master's degrees to access higher pay. It is quite common for a teacher to hold a master's degree and increase their career income by hundreds of thousands of dollars. Let's also dispel the urban myth that districts want to choose teachers without additional college units beyond a bachelor's degree because they are cheaper to hire. I have been around hiring personnel in several districts and never once perceived this to be the case. Districts that you want to work for want to hire the best teachers, period.

If you have a growth mindset, here is what a higher degree can do for you. It can inform your teaching. It can challenge you constructively. It can cultivate your confidence. Ultimately, it can make you better for the countless learners you will instruct. If you are already a successful entrepreneur, pursuing a degree may not be worth it. But for the rest of us (especially teachers), be wise and go back to school.

Action Steps:

> ➢ Take steps to research nearby degree options. Take a step further and draft a plan to accomplish this.

> ➢ If you already have a higher degree, encourage other teachers to take these steps as well.

The Art of The Hook

"When teachers create 'curiosity' in their classrooms, kids start to wonder... when they wonder, they want to learn." - Rick Wormeli

Much like a commercial, movie trailer, or billboard, the lesson hook is meant to grab focus and leave students wanting more. Practically speaking, a hook could come in many forms, including: quotations, activities, games, demonstrations, short videos, pictures, hypotheticals, jokes, excerpts, pop-culture references, or statistics. The hook could be something special, funny, mysterious, shocking, challenging, sad, scary, peculiar, memory-provoking, or thought-provoking. It could bring about feelings of joy, curiosity, sympathy, empathy, annoyance, or even anger.

Strictly speaking, it's not an absolute necessity, but most lessons could benefit from a hook. Hooks are known by different names. Madeline Hunter calls the hook an anticipatory set. The first of "The Five Es" of lesson design is "engage," which is also a hook. It really doesn't take much teacher prep time, and it can draw your students into the lesson, especially your reluctant learners. Brevity is key. This attention-getter could serve several purposes simultaneously, including tying to prior knowledge, referencing past lessons, foreshadowing future ones, or linking content to student interests.

Clearly, a hook can be many things. But not everything is a hook. Announcing, "You'd better pay attention, this is important" is not a great hook. Correcting homework from last night is no hook at all. Neither is taking roll or handling classroom housekeeping or announcements. While there's a definite time and place for these activities, we can do better to draw in our learners with our hooks.

One of my favorite hooks was to place sticky notes or dry erase markers on the desks of certain students before the class entered the room. On the whiteboard, I could have an activity such as listing, matching, solving a riddle, filling in blanks, or making predictions, all of which require student input. If I played my cards right, I could have most students out of their seats and actively participating prior to the opening of the lesson. Closure activities can serve a similar purpose, wrapping up the lesson in a way that is fun, meaningful, and brief.

If you teach multiple subjects, you could benefit from multiple daily hooks. If you teach one subject, you have fewer excuses; you just need one hook to use over and again during your day. The beauty is that there are countless ways to hook students. So, have fun mixing it up and know that daily routines don't have to be dull. Humor, facts, activities, games, clips, and more…find some hooks that work for you and your learners.

Action Steps:

> ➢ **Even if a hook is brief, enhance every lesson by using the hook to creating curiosity and wonder for learning.**

Checking for Understanding and Assessments

"When teachers do formative assessment effectively, students learn at roughly double the rate that they do without it." - Dylan Wiliam

As a rookie teacher, I used to go home and think to myself, "Wow, my students really got it today. They were answering hard questions. They were asking even better ones. What a great teacher I am." It wasn't until the next year that I finally realized I was missing something. Usually only about 5-6 students were locked in and tracking with me on any given day, giving me the impression that all students were locked in and tracking. What about the other 30? I assumed they were tracking with me, but were they?

The truth is, I had no idea if the majority of my students were getting it. Some argue that this is what summative assessments are for. But highly effective teachers have a reasonable idea of what their students know before a big test. The truth is, checking for understanding and formative assessments became life preservers for me, as well as for my students. While I believed I was doing a great job before, actually I was doing my students a disservice and setting them up for failure by not informally assessing along the way. I once heard this helpful metaphor: "When the cook tastes the soup, that's formative assessment; when the customer tastes the soup, that's summative assessment."

There are all sorts of ways to do this. Students can use whiteboards or hold up different color cards to represent answers. Students can self-assess and visually respond using a scale such as thumbs-up-thumbs-down, or fist-to-five. Teachers can also use any number of digital resources to do this as well (Kahoot, Padlet, Stormboard, Pinup, or Google Classroom, to name a few). Checking progress and gauging what they know is at the heart of formative assessment. As the phrase suggests, formative assessment is an ongoing cycle of building up or forming student skills, measuring, and building up some more. It allows the teacher to adjust instruction as needed. Formative assessment means that students are safe and free to risk and make mistakes before and leading up to a real assessment.

If you don't check for understanding, you may be releasing students to work independently and unknowingly set them up to practice incorrectly. Perhaps even more importantly, effective checking for understanding is a top indicator of student success. John Hattie's *Visible Learning* referenced earlier in this book, finds that "teacher estimates of achievement" is a top five indicator of student success (Hattie, 2015). With that in mind, don't wait until the test to find out if they truly get it or if they passed or failed. Set students up for success by measuring their skills and progress along the journey of lessons leading up to the big test. In other words, let the cook taste the soup before the customer does.

Action Steps:

➢ **With every learning objective, make sure your lesson allows for students to "taste the soup" before you formally assess them.**

Fullan's Secrets of Change
for Your Classroom

"Change really isn't as hard as we thought if we capture people's interest and give them enjoyable, worthwhile experiences." - Michael Fullan

Toronto native Michael Fullan has been one of the biggest names in educational leadership for decades. He has written dozens of books, none more impactful than *Six Secrets of Change*. In short, this book promotes positive changes in schools by calling leaders to: love their employees, connect people with purpose, build capacity in employees, recognize that learning *is* the work, be transparent, and develop a sustainable system that transcends and outlasts the leader (Fullan, 2011). As with many broader educational frameworks, this can be adapted to a smaller scale and successfully applied to the classroom setting. I tried Fullan's secrets and found myself addicted.

- As the classroom leader, a teacher can tap into these six secrets to promote positive change in the classroom.

- First, valuing and *loving your students* will establish the right priorities and be the foundation for success in the classroom.

- Second, *purposefully connecting students* with the content and with each other (via collaboration) can open a venue for sharing ideas and best practices, gives teachers a built-in monitoring tool, and aligns individual and group goals for students.

- Third, *building capacity in your students* (e.g. growing in them skills, perseverance, routines, independence, etc.) will reap long-term rewards for you and your students.

- Fourth, a *focus on the work of student learning* requires a healthy balance of consistency and innovation, both for you in lesson-design and for your students in what they produce.

- Fifth, *be transparent with your students*, their parents, and your colleagues. Communicate openly about student data and academic progress.

- Sixth, recognize that you are *establishing an effective system* in which you could be expendable, where a substitute or any future teacher could execute, benefit, or capitalize on what you have done with your students. What a beautiful thing when the teacher, as a result of their effective system, can fade into the background as their students shine!

Secrets of change in education are secrets no more. The wisdom that Fullan offers works at the district level. It works at the school level. There is no reason why it cannot also work in the classroom. Learning how to apply it in your personal context can work for you, too.

Action Steps:

**Apply Fullan's secrets to your work as a teacher
by asking these six questions:**

➢ **Do you love your students?**

➢ **Do you purposefully connect them to their learning?**

➢ **Do you seek to build capacity in them?**

➢ **Is student learning your focus?**

➢ **Are you transparent with them?**

➢ **Does your system work, even if you were absent for a time?**

504s And IEPs In A Nutshell

"Everybody is a genius. But if you judge a fish by its ability to climb a tree, it will live its whole life believing that it is stupid." - Albert Einstein

"Special children need well-trained teachers who used materials adapted to those children's capabilities. They should not be abandoned to state institutions." - Margaret Bancroft, advocate for Special Education (1879)

Not everyone learns the same way, at the same speed, or with the same materials. In past decades, many local, state, and federal laws have been designed to address students with specific struggles, learning needs, or disabilities, few more prevalent than the 1973 Rehabilitation Act. From this law comes the framework for the modern 504 Plan. All classroom teachers should have an adequate understanding of 504s as they will inevitably find students to which this program applies. The following paragraph should not be mistaken for exhaustiveness, but should serve as a starting point.

504s - Stemming from Section 504 of the Rehabilitation Act of 1973, a 504 Plan provides services or changes to the learning environment so that a child can equitably access their education. 504 Plans are also free to the parents of the child, and schools are not reimbursed for services provided. The federal government can take away funding for non-compliance, however. Students qualify if a disability such as physical limitations or attention issues interfere with their ability to learn. The 504 definition for disability is much broader than IDEA, so students who don't qualify for an IEP might still qualify for a 504. Students on a 504 spend their day in the general education environment. A 504 Plan is usually a written document, but doesn't have to be. It lists specific accommodations, supports, or services to assist the child, as well as the individuals responsible to provide them. Common examples of qualifiers for 504 Plans include students with: ADD, ADHD, physical challenges, vision or hearing impairment, dyslexia, severe allergies, diabetes, asthma, or other chronic conditions that impact how students function at school.

Not everyone learns the same way, at the same speed, or with the same materials. In past decades, many local, state, and federal laws have been designed to address students with specific struggles, learning needs, or disabilities; few more prevalent than the 2004 IDEA Act. From this law comes the framework for the modern IEP. All classroom teachers should have an adequate understanding of IEPs as they will inevitably find students to which this program applies. Again, the following is to serve as an adequate starting point.

IEPs - Stemming from the Individuals with Disabilities Education or IDEA Act (2004), an Individualized Education Program or "IEP" is a plan for a child's specialized education experience at school. These programs are free for families as schools are reimbursed with federal funding. To qualify, a child must have one of 13 listed specific learning disabilities (SLDs) which affect their performance or ability to learn or benefit from the general education curriculum. Although the title "Special Education" is going away in some places, students on IEPs usually have allotted time outside the general education environment. These learners often have a specified number of daily or weekly instructional minutes receiving specialized academic instruction (SAI) or other services. These other services might include things like speech, language, counseling, therapy, or adaptive P.E. For students receiving SAI minutes or other services, there are measurable goals attached to them, which are reported at annual IEP meetings. Required at IEP meetings are a parent, a Special Education teacher or case manager, a general education teacher, a district representative, and possibly other service providers. The IEP itself is a written document that keeps track of a student's present levels of performance, annual goals, minutes of service, classroom accommodations and modifications (which applies to both SAI and general education classes), and any accommodations for standardized testing. Students are reevaluated every three years to determine qualification and can be dismissed from an IEP if they no longer qualify.

Action Steps:

> ➤ **In plain terms, practice explaining a 504 Plan and an IEP to a friend or family member that is not involved in education**

Music Is Magical in The Classroom

"When words fail, music speaks." - William Shakespeare

Music is nothing short of magical. Our brains have been hard-wired to associate music with long-term memory. Music has been linked to greater mathematical reasoning, deep emotional recall, and has been known to combat depression. Music has even been shown to reverse some effects of dementia. From the womb to old age, music connects neurons and stimulates minds.

I have seen dozens of ways that music was brought into the classroom with positive results. Here are a few:

- Playing music as students walk in the room as a mood-setter, hook, or something related to the lesson

- Analyzing rhetorical devices in songs (metaphors and similes in Katy Perry's "Firework," Irony in Alanis Morrissette's "Ironic," which students later determined didn't have the best uses of irony, and that was pretty ironic)

- Teaching a deliberate lesson on a music genre, including sample music (jazz was a particular favorite for students as it influenced so many other genres, including Rock and Roll)

- Making up songs for the purpose of helping students recall information

- Teacher strumming on the guitar with ad lib lyrics about the lesson

- Determining the meanings of anti-war songs from the Vietnam War era ("Unknown Soldier," "For What It's Worth," "Fortunate Son," "Born in the U.S.A.," etc.)

- Arranging "rap battles" where students prepared lyrics beforehand and presented to their classmates

- Classical music during a test or study session, "name that tune" for enrichment, music videos to analyze emotion

- Theme songs for each unit of history ("Buffalo Soldier," "Erie Canal," and "Yankee Doodle" came from a list of 30 in a U.S. History class)

- Using Woody Guthrie songs to recap the Dust Bowl and Great Depression

- Breaking down and rewriting lyrics from the musical "Hamilton" in layman's terms in a government class

- P.E. teacher singing tunes aloud to his classes during roll call; usually his songs were themed by the day of the week or current events

- P.E. teacher playing heavy metal renditions of Adele, Enya, and other easy-listening songs for workout time

- P.E. teacher allowing students to bring headphones and listen to the music of their choice while running the mile

With such a powerful, proven learning tool at your disposal, it is time to bring more music into your classroom. It will make you and your students happier, healthier, and help them to learn and to retain information.

Action Steps:

➢ **Estimate how many times you use music in the classroom during the school year. Why not double it?**

Give Them A Glimpse into Your World

"Students learn as much for a teacher as from a teacher." - Linda Darling-Hammond

A sure way to build a bridge between you and your students is to give them a glimpse into your world. You might teach in a community or population that is very familiar to you, very foreign for you, or somewhere in between. In any case, showing them a little bit of who you are humanizes you, and will do wonders in terms of students wanting to work with you and produce for you.

For me, a big hit with students was my "first-days-of-school" slideshow. I took a good 30-minute chunk of time to show my students prearranged pictures and videos of my life. Chronologically, the slideshow included a few baby pictures, pictures of me playing sports when I was their age, pictures of my wife and kids, silly Photoshop projects (some of which they thought were real, like a lightsaber fight with friends), recent globe-trotting to Japan and the Philippines, and pictures of fun times with previous classes. It worked almost too well. I was immediately their favorite teacher and I had hardly done any teaching to earn that title. At the same time, my slideshow earned their trust, gained their respect, set me up as their role model, and previewed the wonderful times we were to experience together that school year. They couldn't wait to learn from me. They couldn't wait to learn *for* me.

I have witnessed other teachers take different approaches to building bridges with students, finding great success as well. Some teachers bring their service dog or other pets, show off special skills (juggling, singing, dancing, acting, cooking), coach or invest in students outside of school, have encouraging talks after class, or offer rewards like lunch-with-the-teacher.

Action Steps:

➢ Use any of these ideas to give students a glimpse into your world. Be warned, however. You had better be prepared to deal with the responsibility of being a favored teacher.

Play A Good Game, Don't Just Talk One!

"Play is really the work of childhood." - Mr. (Fred) Rogers

Freidrich Froebel, who laid the foundation for modern education, says, "play is the highest expression of human development in childhood for it alone is the free expression of what is in a child's soul" (Froebel, 2015). Whether we want to admit it or not, we all compete and play games. Most of us enjoy watching others compete as well. It's what makes video games, game shows, talent shows, sporting events, and music and dance competitions so popular. Through competition we learn, we grow, we adjust, we find uncertainty, and we shape outcomes based on our performances. Competition offers a kind of thrill and opportunity that doesn't exist elsewhere. If you aren't incorporating competition in the classroom, why not?

Some classroom games have little academic value, and others are so rigorous they don't feel much like a game. But the sweet spot between these two poles is vast. Some types of competition require tremendous brain power and others require little. Sometimes teachers do it for the sake of routines or classroom management. Kids come alive with competition. The decade-old trivia game "Jeopardy!" offers a nice template and starting point for classroom competition. The most basic version tallies your score based on correct answers; the harder the question, the more points. This is ever popular since it can cover basic recall questions for any subject. The Jeopardy template can be modified for higher-order thinking, can pit groups of students against each other for higher participation rates, can integrate video, audio, or picture clues, and can make use of student-designed questions and answers. Trivia games like "Beat the teacher," "Who Wants to Be a Millionaire," "Swat-the-answer," "Guess-the-artifact," "Family Feud," or "What's in the bag?" can also be modified to adequately engage or challenge.

"It's all fun and games until someone gets hurt." This adage applies to classroom competition, too. Games should never lead to ridicule, unkindness, bitterness, or the like. Remember that for some cultures that are collectivist, competition is a dirty word. Before, during and after any formal class competition, the whole class (teacher included) is united as a team, striving for academic greatness together. It is important to solidify this in the minds of your students so that they know the purpose of classroom competition and properly contextualize academic games.

Competition in a classroom can go beyond academics and have practical purposes as well. Mini competitions within the day help with routines and management. Competition can bring order out of chaos without having to police students. Positively reinforce the behavior of individuals, rows, or table groups by giving them front-of-the-line passes to lunch or letting them leave first for break. Use a token economy to pit students against students, classes against classes, or offer a single class challenge. Students or classes can fill a jar of marbles, earn points, or collect tickets in order to earn prizes, privileges, pizza, or preferred activities.

Competition lights a fire in all of us, and our students are no exception. Routinely introduce games into your lessons. It can be involved, lengthy, or formal, or it can be short, casual, or improvised. It can go beyond recall, promote critical thinking, require collaboration, or support behavioral expectations. Competition is a thrill that can be used to enhance the learning process. Whatever you do, let them compete! Let the games begin!

Action Steps:

> ➢ **Incorporate competition in upcoming lessons.**
> ➢ **Specifically, design lessons in which students can compete against themselves, against other students, and against you.**

Generations on Staff:
Respect Elders...Youngsters, Too

"In a way, I feel sorry for the kids of this generation. They'll have parents who know how to check browser history." - Unknown

The study of Generations is more art than science. Not everyone agrees on which years mark the start or end of generations. Each generation tends to be about a 20-year period, and cut-offs are often marked by cultural paradigm shifts, such as wars or technological advancements. Also, discussions about generations is mostly an American phenomenon. Some other Western nations might have similar trends and generational cut-offs, but generations from other parts of the world can have vastly different experiences and characteristics. Also, characteristics associated with each generation are largely based on generalities, stereotypes, or collective identities. With these provisos in mind, consider the fact that schools around the world perpetually operate with multiple generations on staff at the same time. In addition, it's important to remember that all generations have their strengths and weaknesses. Here are some points to think about as you go about working with colleagues from varying generations.

The Baby Boom Generation (born mid 1940s-early 1960s) is named for the fact that the years after World War II brought record birthrates for American families. Not all are retired, and as I write, many will continue working for years to come. Boomers have much to offer. In general, Boomers greatly value work and career, are competitive, optimistic, youthful, and skeptical of institutions. If you are a Millennial or Gen Z, remember that Boomers raised you. Have respect for your elders.

Generation X, also called the MTV Generation (born early 1960s to early 1980s), is called such because the X variable represents the limitless potential and unknown value of this post-Baby Boom generation. Many

Gen Xers have a strong desire for stability, creativity, and outside-the-box thinking. They are cynical, casual, informal, independent, self-reliant, and fun. These descriptors are especially true at work. They love art, they love to rock, and they love to be awesome.

The Millennial Generation (born early 1980s to early 2000s) is also called Generation Y since it follows Generation X. The term *Millennial* refers to the fact that this generation was born just before the year 2000. Millennials were largely raised by helicopter parents and therefore struggle with entitlement. They have a healthy balance of work and home life, are tech savvy, committed friends, conscious consumers, well-read, idealistic, and pragmatic. They are the best time-managers yet and can get stuff done.

Generation Z refers to anyone born from 2003 - 2020ish. Several other telling names refer to this generation, including: iGeneration, Pluralist Generation, New Lost Generation, Generation@, Net-Generation, Digital Native Generation, Homeland Generation, Scholars Generation, & #Gen. Gen Z is the most diverse generation yet. They were born into technology and have been tweeting, texting, FaceTiming, and Snapping since infancy. They are not only cynical, obnoxious, spoiled, and disrespectful, but also wicked-smart, realistic, innovative, and confident. If any group is equipped for distance learning and virtual lessons, it's this one. Watch out, they *really* will get stuff done.

All generations bring immense gifts to the table. All have their pitfalls, as well. There is no "worst" generation; no, not even the young ones. There is no "greatest" generation; the G.I. Generation that fought in World War II already took that title. Admittedly, the above descriptions are very much based on generalizations. But it is important to know who you are working with. Be respectful to each other. Learn from each other. Honor and value each other. Journey together.

Action Steps:

➢ Cross-reference your generation's stereotypes with your own tendencies.

➢ Identify an area of growth related to your generation and your tendencies.

➢ Compliment a colleague from another generation for some of their strengths.

Tech That Enhances and Advances

"Technology will never replace great teachers, but technology in the hands of great teachers is transformational." - George Couros

In second grade, I took a test with my classmates and somehow qualified for G.A.T.E. or "Gifted and Talented Education." This granted me access to more rigorous instruction. But practically speaking, the only perk was that I missed part of class each week to go to a computer lab. This was 1991, and the part-time computer teacher with six Macintosh devices in a storage closet-turned computer lab were novelties. I remember games like "Oregon Trail," "Odell Lake," and "Incredible Machine." The academic benefit was negligible. Today, it is hard to imagine a classroom without devices. In the early 1990s, some leaders had the vision to use technology for learning. Today, some are just as adept at exploring the learning opportunities that are offered by devices. Some are not. It depends on the classroom.

Several years ago, when districts began going "one-to-one" (one device per child), some teachers considered a set of Chromebooks or iPads to be intimidating or burdensome, and expensive devices went unused. Other teachers only looked at what was formerly done with pencil and paper, and then went about having students do the same tasks with screens and keyboards. The lessons were no more than tech doppelgangers of former lessons. This was often to the disservice of students as studies have shown that, brains work harder with screens and students tend to learn and recall better with pencil and paper, especially with numbers (Wastlund, 2007). Maria Montessori was right all along when she said, "What the hand does, the mind remembers." Parents and educators were divided on whether tech in the classroom was a good thing or not.

Then there were trailblazers. Visionary teachers asked questions like, "How can we go beyond technology that *replaces* learning, and get to technology that *enhances* learning?" Dr. Ruben Puentedura's SAMR Model frames the discussion well. SAMR stands for technology that *substitutes* (no functional change), *augments* (functional change), *modifies* (significant task redesign), and *redefines* classroom tasks (new tasks previously inconceivable) (Puentadura, 2015). Considering health risks associated with excessive screen time, this discussion is now more important than ever. If you only use screens to substitute what your students already did on paper, why are you doing it? Either move on to tech that modifies and redesigns tasks or else go back to paper and pencil. The answer isn't more screen time, it's more effective screen time. Use technology to do something that you never could have done before with pencil and paper.

Many teachers were already reaping benefits of an innovative approach before COVID. And these technologically innovative educators were better equipped to adapt to seasons of distance learning. Whether at home on in the classroom, devices in the hands of students have enormous implications on differentiation, STEAM, personalized or blended learning, timely feedback, collaboration, communication, cultural responsiveness, assessment, coding, and more. The device boom also means greater access to supplemental materials such as educational YouTubers like the John Green, Minute Physics, Crash Course Science, or TED Talks. The technology train is going fast. Do your students a favor and get on board, keeping the SAMR model in mind as you look to do things previously unheard of in a classroom setting.

Action Steps:

➢ **Review your approach to classroom tech, making sure there is good reason to do what you do.**

➢ **Identify ways to use technology to redefine learning; asking students to accomplish things that were never possible with pencil and paper.**

Best Practices for Solid Sub Plans

*"All right, listen up, y'all. I'm your substitute teacher Mr. Garvey.
I taught school for 20 years in the inner city, so don't even think
about messing with me. Y'all feel me? Okay, let's take the roll
here." - Keegan-Michael Key's "Substitute Teacher" skit*

I hate writing sub plans. I would rather come in with pneumonia than write sub plans; and I did once. I have known many a teacher who feels the same. It's not that there aren't great substitute teachers out there, because there are. I just don't like that it takes me an hour to make plans. I don't like it when a day's worth of instruction is out of my hands. I also don't like cleaning up the mess (real or imagined) when I return; trying to figure out what was accomplished, who acted up, and following through with whatever still needs to be done. It took me a few years of learning the hard way to figure it out, but there is a better way.

I boil down many of the best practices I have come across into a simple, three-part motto: preparation, simplicity, follow-through.

Preparation - Life happens, and we are going to miss work sometimes, especially if you have children of your own. For the longest time, I didn't think ahead about missing days of work or arranging plans for a substitute to work with my students. When the time came, I phoned it in by either hurriedly putting something together at the last minute or relying on colleagues to borrow a stand-alone lesson. Both scenarios brought unnecessary stress to either me or my colleagues, and neither was great for my students. I finally took a page from a teacher friend who had a folder of prepared "go-to" lesson plans. In case of emergency, I had to do little more than point them to the appropriate folder. Each of these lesson plans was universal in nature, so they could be used at any point in the school year. The lessons went beyond busy work, too. Each one appropriately challenged, enriched, and delighted my students. Do a solid for your students, your sub, and your colleagues. Create a folder with pre-arranged sub-plans.

Simplicity - At first, I spent a great deal of time writing very specific, detailed plans, expecting the substitute to do just as I would have. This was not only unrealistic, but it was unfair to the professional charged with covering my class. No one teaches exactly like me and no one should. The more complicated I made my directions, the more I was taking away their freedom. I have learned to keep my plans thorough, yet simple. Doing so will set up your substitute for success. Simple plans will let your sub put some of their own creativity and strengths into the lesson and get better cooperation and results from your students. Ultimately, if your students and you have established norms and expectations, they are capable of flourishing without you for a time.

Follow-through - Students quickly figure out if you mean what you say. I worked at a school where subs were eaten alive and students typically got away with it. I also worked at a school where the standard consequence for any misbehavior with a sub was calculatingly harsh. You can guess which school had more success in terms of student behavior with their subs. Ask subs to leave a list of students who were particularly helpful or particularly challenging. Then, make sure you follow up with appropriate steps (consequences or rewards). Be the authority figure with a reputation for following through. Students will respect you more for it in the end.

Find some variation of preparation, simplicity and follow-through that works for you and your students. Doing so with make your life easier, allow your substitute to work more effectively, and allow your students to learn at a high rate even in your absence.

Action Steps:

> **When it comes to sub plans, make your work easier and allow student-learning to continue in your absence by addressing your preparation, simplicity, and follow-through.**

Anecdotes and Analogies:
Give Students A Shot at It

*"You know what takes longer than a kid telling
a story? Nothing." - Unknown*

*"I like having conversations with kids. Grownups never
ask me what my third favorite reptile is." - Unknown*

When I first explain Newton's Laws of Motion to a group of students, I use some unusual examples to demonstrate. One example involved a slow-motion sprint between me and the smallest student. We pretended to race toward each other, preparing for a collision. We would freeze right before the collision, and I would pose a question, "For every action, there is an equal and opposite reaction, so what happens next?" Students were eager to learn more.

Use go-to examples to your advantage. I had countless other anecdotes and analogies that worked to draw students in and make learning come alive in my classroom, and I'm sure you have countless examples as well. Some students can visualize, conceptualize, and make connections on their own, but most of them will benefit greatly from your examples and from the mental pictures you paint.

Always be on the look-out for new examples and stories to help students access curriculum. Sometimes examples grow stale or dated. Sometimes we stumble upon better ways to explain things to our students. Enhancing our go-to examples can be not only be done by lesson-planning with colleagues, observing other lessons, and dialoging with your students, but also through regular life occurrences such as weekend outings, watching the news, or reading a book. Inspiration, ideas, and examples for teaching can come from anywhere. Keep yours fresh.

Don't forget to also leave room for your students to make connections and develop anecdotes and analogies during the learning process. Doing this enhances student learning and allows them to practice thinking critically. I still remember being asked by my high school world history teacher to come up with a fresh metaphor for the British relationship with their former Indian colony. While most students went with some variation of a mother/child metaphor, I likened it to a lucrative company (England) inheriting warehouses full of materials (India). I have asked similar things of my students as I love the way metaphor development challenges students and gets their creativity flowing.

Anecdotes and analogies can get many students to the point of "ah-ha!" There's nothing like the feeling a teacher gets when a student finally grasps a previously incomprehensible concept. Illustrations and examples can serve as your catalysts.

Action Steps:

- ➤ **Lean on and expand your favorite anecdotes and analogies.**
- ➤ **Look for new ones.**
- ➤ **Let your students have a shot at generating them, too.**

Confident Humility

"The mark of a true hero is humility." - Master Shifu

At first glance, "confident humility" seems oxymoronic. However, for a teacher, it is the idyllic place to live. Strike the right balance between confidence and humility, and your students will follow you. Adults will follow you. This is true for first-year educators as well as thirtieth-year ones.

If you are a classroom teacher, you are not simply leading a classroom full of students. You are also leading others on staff, if not formally, then at least by example. To lead students and colleagues, confidence is a prerequisite. Now, let's be clear; confidence is not arrogance. Arrogance doesn't listen to ideas, doesn't notice others, and is closed-minded. Arrogance is repulsive and anyone can smell it on you. Rather, confidence is admirable. It is demonstrating conviction and reassuring others that you are going somewhere worth going.

Humility is non-negotiable for a classroom teacher as well. Humility, not to be confused with feebleness, is to be respected in a leader. Socrates once said, "I am the wisest man alive, for I know one thing, and that is that I know nothing." It's a bit flippant, but he makes a great point about humility. No one will ever truly be a legitimate "know-it-all." Humility means you listen, notice, learn, consider, value, and respect other people and their ideas. Your confident humility allows you to admit when you're wrong. Confident humility also speaks truth with grace when *they* are wrong.

Finding a balance of being both confident and humble is the key to moving forward as an educational leader. For instance, having a growth mindset requires confidence to recognize that you can learn, improve, and contribute. In much the same way, it requires humility to recognize your *need* to learn, to improve, and to contribute.

Action Steps:

> ➢ Some err toward arrogance. Some err toward timidity.
>
> ➢ If you don't know where you are on the spectrum, ask someone who can give you an honest answer and strive to find a balance as a confident and humble leader.

Practice, Feedback, Retakes, and Testing on Purpose

"The most powerful single modification that enhances achievement is feedback." - John Hattie

"Learners need endless feedback more than they need endless teaching." - Grant Wiggins

If you think the purpose of an assessment is to reward high performers with a good grade and penalize low performers with a bad one, you are only seeing part of the picture. A test should not punish, should not be obligatory, and should not be done because "that's how it has always been done." The purpose of an assessment is to let students show what they know or what they can do, and to offer feedback. What many educators don't realize is that this is something learners need daily.

I used to teach my tail off, including lots of stand-and-deliver lectures, and then experience extreme disappointment with the resulting grades on unit exams. Of course, I had no idea how they would do because I never bothered to check in with them along the way. I didn't let them practice. I didn't offer much feedback. I just taught...or so I thought. Formative assessment and feedback were largely absent from my lessons. John Hattie, a sage on formative assessment, wisely calls teachers to "know thy impact." It took me a few years to notice that I hadn't bothered to measure my impact on students or monitor their progress. What's more, I didn't make necessary adjustments to my teaching as a result of that progress.

In fact, if you use informal (formative) assessments during lessons leading up to a larger test or exam, there should be few surprises when the formal (summative) assessment arrives. I'm not talking so much about your *students* being surprised as I'm talking about the *teacher* being surprised by the results. If formative assessments and timely feedback regularly occur, the teacher should have a good idea of how their students will perform before the summative assessment takes place.

What educators call formative assessment, Mark Rober calls "The Super Mario Effect." Rober, a YouTuber, blogger, TED-talker, and former NASA scientist, explains that he played video games like Super Mario to gain mastery, not worrying about how many times he failed in the process. No one cares to discuss when they lost a life as Mario fell down the abyss. Instead they care to talk about how they beat Bowser. Rober's Super Mario Effect should find parallels in our classrooms.

Students greatly benefit from feedback, not only on formative assessments, but on summative assessments as well. With few exceptions, I'm a huge fan of test corrections, retakes, and the like. This practice encourages students to see the learning process as fluid and to allow them to purposefully reengage with the content, not to mention the corollary lessons on stick-to-itiveness and work ethic. Unless you know a student is taking advantage of your test retake policy, or you really want your grades to reflect responsibility instead of content, only good things can come from having them revisit the material on an exam.

Action Steps:

➢ **In the context of your teaching assignment, evaluate how you use formative assessments to prepare students for summative assessments.**

➢ **Apply to Super Mario Effect analogy to your students as they improve their skills, and share the analogy with them as well.**

Earning Your "Street Cred"

"Street credit is the points you get for doing something impressive and bold. The more street credit you have the cooler you are." - Urban Dictionary

I love basketball, and I'm not too bad at it, even if I do say so myself. When I worked with younger grades, I would play with them at recess, dribbling around their backs, picking their pockets, and dazzling them with fancy passes, layups, and such. I could even throw down a dunk from time to time. When I worked with high schoolers, I would go head-to-head with them at lunch. Why did I do this, you ask? It wasn't to boost my ego. In fact, I worked hard to help the kiddos on my team score, and I preferred when the game came down to a last shot. The reason I joined in was to bond with the students. I did it to earn my street credit. I did it to build relationships. I can't tell you how many times I bonded with the most difficult learners when other teachers had given up. If it wasn't basketball, I looked for another way in. It might take some time. It might take outside-the-box thinking. But with any student, there are always ways to connect.

One of my more extreme examples was a rap battle with an 8th grader who was a bona fide gang member. Some might call this "code switching." It was more of a polite rap exchange than a true rap battle, and admittedly, I snagged my lyrics from an old Outkast song that I had memorized instead of making them up on the spot. My opponent didn't know. It didn't matter because it earned me my street cred. We benefited from a valuable learning partnership for the rest of the year.

Teachers earn their street cred with students in any number of ways. It can depend on student or teacher variables such as age, gender, special needs, cultural considerations, interests, or hobbies. I've seen teachers who were horrible basketball players take the same approach I did by playing ball at recess. Wisely, they did not take themselves too seriously, yet they had similarly positive results with their students. I also remember an administrative team early in my career produce a short music video for the student body. It was intentionally ridiculous, and they made fools of themselves, but they found greater success working with students afterward. I've seen teachers get down and dirty with art lessons, run the mile with classes in P.E., or pull out the guitar to serenade, entertain, or amuse their students. Whatever they are, use your gifts, talents, and interests to build bridges with students. Or go out on a limb and try something that you aren't particularly good at. There are many ways to earn your street credit and strengthen the learning bond with your students. Explore some of them.

Action Steps:

> **Evaluate how you use "street cred" to build relationships with your students.**

> **Think outside the box to connect to those with whom you have the most difficulty connecting.**

Gradual Release of Responsibility

"You haven't taught it unless they've learned it." - Doug Lemov

We expect our students to do all sorts of amazing things. They need our help to get there, and not just our directions. They need our models, scaffolding, help from peers, sentence frames, and plenty of encouragement. What they need even more is for their teacher to hand over the keys. The reason why is because teachers already have the knowledge or have mastered the skill. Over time it becomes the responsibility of the student to have the knowledge or master the skill. Through a process popularly called "gradual release of responsibility," the role of the teacher is to deliberately build capacity and steadily get them to the goal. And even when students experience great success in our classrooms, they can reach new heights, we can give them greater responsibility, provide them with more tools, and set fresh challenges in front of them.

Gradual release of responsibility or "GRR" can include the teacher showing students how to do something, then asking them to do it in groups or with partners, then letting them do it by themselves. But it doesn't have to be solely that recipe. Checking for understanding is a crucial piece that must be done with fidelity. For instance, if students practice incorrectly in groups, don't let them move on to independent practice where they would only continue to practice incorrectly. You would only know this if you have been monitoring their progress and formally assessing along the way. Use tools to survey the room before moving on with GRR. If they aren't getting it, you may need to reteach, adjust instruction, or address common mistakes.

GRR is something that happens on a macro scale as you survey your whole class, on a micro scale as you work with individual students, and everything in between. GRR occurs throughout the year, as we develop aptitude in our students so that they can do better work, build greater stamina, and work with more independence. GRR happens throughout a unit or grading period as students improve their scores, set high scores, and apply new skills. GRR also happens in individual lessons when we progress through "I do, we do, you do" prior to releasing students for independent work.

Gradual release of responsibility is a pattern for student learning and is vital to efficiently push your students to higher heights. It happens each lesson. It happens throughout a unit. It happens over the course of a school year. Rome wasn't built in a day, but it *was* built gradually.

Action Steps:

> ➤ **Survey the room.**
> ➤ **Gather small groups to give added challenges or support.**
> ➤ **Work with students individually.**
> ➤ **Set them up for success by using gradual release of responsibility to build capacity in your students.**

Teacher Professionalism 101

"If you don't know what is going on, you fake it. Just smile and nod. That will get you far." - Ken Poppers

If you get paid to teach, then you're a *pro* by definition. You are a professional; this is your profession. To ensure you are as such, consider these themes of professionalism.

The Law - Know which laws apply to you and to your job. Certainly, these include your teacher contract, district board policy, and applicable government education codes. The contracts, policies, and codes were written on purpose and are meant to protect you, your students, and others, as well as to support education in general. At least have a working knowledge of the laws so that you don't cross them and so you'll recognize if someone else puts you in a compromising position (whether misguided or uninformed).

Dress code - You can be yourself, express your personality, be a hipster, be a conformist, or anywhere in between, all without conceding your professionalism. Some schools expect a certain standard of dress and other schools are laxer in expectations for attire. In any case, you are in the spotlight each day with students and adults who make assumptions and draw conclusions. Find a way to be yourself while also representing your school and your profession with class.

Boundaries - Being entrusted with children is the ultimate compliment. Primary grade students can be knee huggers, but as a rule, physical contact should be absent from your student interactions. It's also not a good idea to be shut in a room with a lone student. If you ever find yourself in that position, at least stand at an open door so that you are visible to others. You have been trusted with kids. Be exceptionally vigilant.

Digital presence - With the advent of social media, it would not be reasonable to expect teachers to abandon these platforms completely. It would be reasonable, however, to expect teachers to be prudent. Some useful guidelines include not "friending" your students, not detailing your theme park adventures while using sick days, and not posting potentially disreputable material (e.g. offensive political posts, indecent pictures, questionable activities, etc.). You don't just represent yourself, but your institution and a noble profession.

Communication norms - Get back to people in a timely manner, be respectful, assume the best of people, and kindly speak your truth. You don't need to respond to parent emails every 15 minutes, but it is reasonable to respond within a 24-hour period. Keep in mind that tones can be misconstrued in text or email. If prickly emails go back and forth more than a couple times, it's probably time to pick up the phone. If you have physical access, walking over and talking in person can be remarkably effective. For sensitive situations, email works sometimes, the phone is better, face to face is better still.

Responsibilities - The professional obligations of a teacher go well-beyond the classroom. Be punctual and present for staff meetings, team meetings, IEPs, parent conferences, Open House, professional development, and duties, just to name a few. You are giving lasting impressions and are allowing other stakeholders to make judgments and draw conclusions about you and your institution with your presence.

Team player mentality - Teaching can be isolating, but teachers should not be an island. Most faculties have layers of defined teams and all teachers are part of a teams in some way. Be a team player, have an open mind, collaborate, contribute, encourage. This is especially crucial for beginning teachers. Oftentimes, how a new teacher operates with their team informs decisions regarding tenure or permanent status more than does their actual performance in the classroom.

The Golden Rule - Treat others as you want to be treated. In the final analysis, no advice on professionalism would be complete without a reference to The Golden Rule. This rule is the embodiment of professionalism. The Golden Rule should hold true in your interaction with students, colleagues, bosses, parents, and anyone else who enters your professional world.

Action Steps:

➢ **Be a pro by scrutinizing your professionalism as it relates to the law, dress code, boundaries, digital presence, communication norms, responsibilities, team player mentality, and The Golden Rule.**

Major in The Majors

"All states and school will have challenging and clear standards of achievement and accountability for all children, and effective strategies for reaching those standards." - U.S. Department of Education

"The main thing is to keep the main thing the main thing." - Stephen Covey

I used to make quite the impressive cover page for my units. It served as a comprehensive unit study guide. It had 30-40 key terms. It had a dozen main ideas and a dozen key questions to match. It used 8-point font, leaving room on the back for students to look up scores of definitions. It was killer, but it was killing my students, too. By the end of the year, I couldn't part from most of the content, since it was "so important," so I created a final exam study guide with well over 200 questions, from which I would choose about 100 to put on the real test. Despite all of my diligence, final exam scores were disappointing. Two things were happening that I didn't realize at the time. For one, I fell victim to the law of diminishing return. For two, I had a serious expectation problem.

A more realistic expectation for my students was to significantly whittle down my lists of key terms, ideas, and questions for each unit. I still had the option to incorporate the rest of the lists without it overwhelming my students. For one, I could assign a portion of the most important terms, and then ask students to choose a portion of the remaining. I could even leave the rest for enrichment or extra credit opportunities. I asked myself, what are the main things I want *every* student to come away with? Then, what is the next group of things I want *most* students to come away with? Finally, what are the other things I want *some* students to come away with?

Secondary teachers often have one set of guiding content standards. Primary teachers have many. I knew my content-standards backwards and forwards, as all teachers should. I loved my curriculum and wanted so badly for my students to get it all. But as much as we may love the curriculum and strive to cram it all into their brains, we must be practical. There are clear ways to differentiate for our most motivated students while reigning in expectations for the majority. Major in the majors and be creatively flexible with the rest.

Action Steps:

- ➤ **Practice setting realistic expectations for teaching and learning.**
- ➤ **For the next unit or series of lessons, list what all students must come away with, what most students should come away with, and what some advanced students might additionally come away with.**

Dealing with Administrators

"Always be humble and kind." - Tim McGraw

"Leaders who do not act dialogically, but insist on imposing their decisions, do not organize people, they manipulate them." - Paulo Freire

Teachers and administrators. Administrators and teachers. Sometimes they get along. Sometimes not so much. Having spent many years on both sides of this divide, I have some pragmatic insight to share.

First, both positions, classroom teacher and school administrator, deserve enormous respect. And because these two professions are in positions of great power and responsibility in leading students, countless decisions are made each day. Once I heard someone say that, "teachers make more day-to-day decisions than brain surgeons." Probably true. The same is true for administrators. Inevitably, the volume of decisions being made by both teachers and administrators means that sometimes mistakes are made. Therefore, tremendous grace and humility is needed on each side.

Teaching is the greatest profession in the history of the world. Being on stage with a classroom full of eyes waiting for your lead every day is an immense calling, full of responsibility and significance. Many teachers are wonderful and priceless. Some teachers can be notoriously obstinate, difficult to work with, and resistant to change. My craft as a teacher improved most when I was reflective, admitted mistakes, and allowed my administrators to give me fresh perspective and genuine constructive criticism regarding my teaching.

Across the hall, school administrators are in a position to have a considerable impact on teaching and learning culture. They are tasked with leading teachers and many other working professionals in the school setting. Good administrators lead with wisdom, discernment, and have a lasting positive influence. Some administrators can be egotistical, misguided, or even harmful. Some of my greatest seasons of growth as an administrator was when I was reflective, had vulnerable conversations, and received authentic feedback from the teachers I trusted.

Administrators and teachers work in the same location, but that doesn't mean they always work together. Just as teachers must get students on board to move them forward, administrators have a similar approach with their respective teaching staffs. Working together is better than working separately or contrarily. This is true both anecdotally and through research. One of the best things an administrator could hear from a teacher is, "What is your vision and how do I fit? How can I help?" Some of the best things teachers can hear are, "How do you want to grow? What do you want to work on? What are your goals? How can I help?" Both jobs are enormously valuable. Whichever side you are on, always remember to have respect, and always be humble and kind.

Action Steps:

> ➤ **At an appropriate time and in an appropriate setting, ask your administrator about their vision and how you might help bring it to fruition.**

Educational Buzz Words

"Don't throw out buzz words without really knowing what is going on behind it." - Salman Khan

I can't tell you how many times I went into a meeting and heard educational acronyms and phrases that were foreign to me. Sometimes I faked it, other times I asked about them later, but it still would have been best to know what people were talking about instead of having to puzzle it out. Below is an organized directory of common buzz words, phrases, and acronyms used in education. This is by no means an exhaustive list, and a list like this is also subject to change as years advance. Some educational buzz words lose their buzz, some are pedantic, and others are here to stay. Here are thirty such words and phrases to consider.

Benchmarks - a point of reference against which something is compared or assessed

Best Practices - procedures that are accepted or promoted as being most effective

Blended Learning - a combination of online resources with traditional classroom methods

Checking for Understanding - measuring student knowledge or skills before moving forward

Closure - recapping a main idea or learning objective for a lesson or learning segment

Common Core - the essential standards adopted by most states to develop college-ready skills in students

Cooperative Learning - an approach to teaching that requires students to work together to complete tasks

Culturally Responsive Pedagogy - Knowing your students and taking their cultures into consideration while teaching

Differentiated Instruction - a framework that provides different students with different ways of learning

Flipped Classroom - reversing traditional learning by delivering content at home and engaging content in class

Formative Assessment - informal evaluations of student comprehension, needs, and progress

Gradual Release of Responsibility - devolving teacher responsibility, increasingly giving independence to the learner

Growth Mindset - believing knowledge and skills aren't fixed, but grow through hard work, good strategies, and attitude

Higher Order Thinking Skills (HOTS) - beyond recall, asking students to apply, analyze, synthesize, and evaluate material

IEP - From the 2004 IDEA Act, a specialized school experience plan for a child with an identified learning disability

Inquiry-based - presenting problems and scenarios while asking students to be their own investigative agents

Instructional Rounds - classroom visits aimed to recognize and develop high-quality instruction

Learning Objective - The target or goal for students to achieve though the lesson, often knowledge or skills

Personalized Learning - pedagogy, curriculum, and environments tailored to meet individual learner needs or interests

Primary Source Document - raw materials of history; the text or media from an event or time period under study

Professional Development (PD) - coursework, conferences, or other learning to maintain credentials or improve practices

Professional Learning Community - educators collaborating regularly to share expertise to improve teaching and learning

Progress Monitoring - considering student growth or development and adjusting instruction accordingly

Rigor - learning experiences that are academically, intellectually, and/or personally challenging

Scaffolding - providing support that allows students to build capacity during instruction as skills/concepts are introduced

Specialized Academic Instruction (SAI) - instruction that is separate from the general education learning environment

Standards Based Unit of Study - using standards as the foundation for curriculum, instruction, and assessment

Structured Student Interaction - purposely planned opportunities for accountable language production during a lesson

Summative Assessment - a formal evaluation of student comprehension at the end of an instructional unit

Zone of Proximal Development - the difference between what a learner can do (unaided) and what they can't yet do

504 Plan - From the 1973 Rehabilitation Act, a provision of services or changes so a child equitably accesses education

Action Steps:

> - **Make a copy of this list.**
> - **Add to it as new or recurring buzz words and terms come about in your profession.**
> - **Share it with a new teacher.**

Research with A Twist: Scaffolds, Originality, Choice

*"Variety is the very spice of life, that gives it
all its flavor." - William Cowper*

A common theme at any grade level and in any content area, is the ability to find information and do something with it. We ask our students to research topics and do all sorts of things with the information. We ask them to summarize, analyze, synthesize, hypothesize, question positions, find evidence, site sources, chew it up, digest it, spit it out, hang it on a graphic organizer, or put a bow on it. Some of our students are capable and highly motivated to learn by independently researching information and doing meaningful things with it. Other students can get lost in the library, in a single book, or with too many tabs open on their web browser. Still others don't yet have the ability, don't know where to begin, or won't even try. I'd like to offer some solutions by way of four words: scaffolding, relevance, originality, choice.

Scaffolding refers to support and guidance for your students and could come in many forms, including offering sentence or paragraph frames, modeling tasks that are expected of students, giving a list of credible websites from which to choose, or providing accessible, grade-level informational text. Instead of just giving general directions and a device, consider how and where your students will find the information, as well as the specific parameters in which you expect them to operate.

Relevance is a key piece if you want highly motivated students. If your most challenging students were to ask, "What's in it for me?" what would your response be? Your answer should have nothing to do with their grade or report card. The most effective teachers foresee "relevance roadblocks" early and clear them out of the way by letting students know why they should care. This can be done by using an effective hook, by having direct conversations about the importance of the research, or by connecting the skills or the information to student interests or to real-life situations.

Originality can change everything. Reading, digesting, and writing a summary paragraph isn't the only way to research. Making a poster isn't the only type of product. Student creations can include all sorts of things, such as: songs, poems, videos, pictures, comic strips, diagrams, audio recordings, or graphic organizers. One of my favorite examples is what I call the "Historical Stick Figure." This dolled up version of a graphic organizer asks students to find information for 10 body parts of a stick figure, each relating to an aspect of the spotlighted person. For example, the *brain* section asks about their ideas, the *right hand* about their strengths, the *mouth* about a famous quotation, and the *Achilles' heel* about their weaknesses or challenges. The Historical Stick Figure is an example of research with a twist.

Choice is among the greatest motivators for our students. Give them options with their research and they will be far more excited to jump in. These choices could be about how or where they find their information, about what they choose to research, or about how they digest and hang the information in the end. To use the Historical Stick Figure as an example, students may elect to find the information from a variety of locations, could work from a list of famous people, or may be permitted to choose 8 of the 10 body parts to complete instead of doing them all.

Action Steps:

➤ **Use one of the scaffolding strategies mentioned above to better support students.**

➤ **Inspect tasks given to students with an eye for relevance.**

➤ **Take steps to turn graphic organizers into something unique in order to aid the learning process.**

➤ **Make sure to give students plenty of choices when it comes to their learning.**

In the Digital Age, Embrace A Real-Life Conversation

"What we've got here is a failure to communicate."
- Strother Martin (Cool Hand Luke)

All too often, well-meaning teachers blur real-life conversations with electronic ones. Text messaging is not the same as face-to-face discussion. An email is very different from a phone call. Think about these differences as they apply to your communication with those on campus (co-workers in particular) as well as those off campus (parents in particular).

Among staff members, there are good reasons to rely on electronic communication in the school setting. For one, you likely have had face-to-face interactions with the people you are emailing, giving your electronic communication clearer meaning. For two, communication within a school can be more time sensitive, may need to go to broader groups, or may simply need to relay basic information. However, face-to-face or phone conversations with on-site colleagues are irreplaceable when tone, complexity, or sensitive information are potential concerns.

The guidelines are equally distinctive when it comes to parent communication. Electronic communication may work well for informational pieces or for mass emails. Often when you need to communicate something to a parent about a delicate issue such as grades or behavior, a phone call is the *right* call. The risk of misread tones decreases significantly with phone calls. This practice, particularly early in the school year, sets up for a year of better communication with parents. You might even rely on email later with greater communicative success, having already established a working relationship with a parent on the phone. And even in cases where you may want to document parent communication (e.g. overcoming language barriers or establishing paper trails), you can always talk on the phone first and send a follow-up email saying something like, "It was great talking to you about such-and-such this morning, let me know if I can help with anything else."

I finally got on board and embraced parent phone calls when I put teacher/parent communication in a teacher/student framework. I asked myself this question, "Would I be an effective communicator with my students if I just sat behind my computer all day and fired off emails or messages to them via their devices instead of talking to them?" Obviously not. As much as I initially resisted having face-to-face conversations or making parent phone calls, I recognized that working with staff and working with parents was a vital part of my job. I sometimes learned this the hard way, but eventually was reminded of the power in real-life communication. I've said this before, but it bears repeating: tone is easily misinterpreted in an email or text message. Whenever you can, meet up or pick up the phone; there is great value in a real conversation.

Action Steps:

➢ **This month, instead of sending what would normally be an email, make it a point to talk to three colleagues face-to-face or to talk with three parents on the phone.**

Don't Get Mad, Get Glad! It's Good for Everyone

"Children who have learned to be comfortably dependent can become not only comfortably independent, but can also become comfortable with having people depend on them. They can lean, or stand and be leaned upon, because they know what a good feeling it can be to feel needed." - Fred Rogers

Debates rage over how best to address English language learners. Do we mainstream or offer separate instruction? Do we place an intensive focus on language while other subjects fall by the wayside? Do we fully immerse ELD students in general education classrooms and hope that language sticks? Something in between? Something else? Enter Project GLAD.

Guided Language Acquisition Design or "GLAD" is an English Language Development (ELD) instructional model that promotes academic language and high achievement for English language learners. It was developed by Marcia Brechtel and Linnea Haley in the 1980s, rising to prominence throughout California. It was promoted by the U.S. Department of Education, receiving federal grants by the 1990s. Today, it is used in hundreds of districts, both nationally and internationally. Formal training includes a seven-day intensive commitment, complete with overviews, lesson observations, discussions, debriefs, and planning time.

Before we dive into the GLAD methodology, two points need to be made right off the bat. First, most of these strategies aren't new. They have been around for ages and have been known by different names. When you are exposed to GLAD strategies, you may be saying, "Hey, I already do something like that!" GLAD is simply the award-winning model that tied it all together. Second, these strategies work for English learners, but they are good for *all* language learners. Here are a handful of well-known GLAD strategies to consider adding to your repertoire.

Cognitive Content Dictionary - learning new vocabulary via critical thinking. Using a chart, learners will predict, define, draw pictures, create sentences, and find synonyms for new words. Asking students to create visuals and write sentences for key terms in content areas like history and science are great ways to promote academic language and critical thinking.

Pictorial Input Chart - an image with empty boxes for students to input information. The scaffolding can vary greatly. For instance, it may be completely blank, or it may already provide content headings or sentence frames. This is a fantastic strategy for comparing and contrasting data such as animals, key figures, math formulas, parts of speech, and more.

Expert Groups - also called a jigsaw, students break up information and are responsible for processing different chunks of it. Next, they will master the information and teach it to classmates. Using an activity such as a gallery walk is a great way to get students up and moving around the room to learn from each other in this way.

Process Grid - universal graphic organizer to hang information in columns and rows. A teacher often provides the framework (titles) and asks students to fill in the rest. This is easy to modify for students of varying capacities. Teachers could fill in one example from each row or column to provide a model for students to work from.

Cooperative Strip Paragraph - students form groups to create sentences on a larger paper, which combine with sentences of other groups to make a paragraph. Collective revising takes place as a class. Teachers can cut the sentences into smaller chunks as well for the rearranging process.

Action Steps:

> ➢ **GLAD strategies are good for all language learners.**
> ➢ **Add one of these strategies to your toolbox and use it during an upcoming lesson.**

Grading 101: What No One Teaches in Teacher School

"When students cheat on exams it's because our school system values grades more than students value learning." - Neil deGrasse Tyson

The gradebook topic is one that is notoriously passed over in most teaching programs and teachers are left to figure it out on their own. What is the purpose of grading? Why do elementary schools tend to use three-point rubrics for their benchmarks? Who decided on the 5-letter grade scale for secondary schools? Who says letters A, B, C, and D correspond to 10% ranges and F covers a 60% range? How much should assignments be worth? How many assignments should be posted to the gradebook each week? Am I grading based on students' performance and mastery, or based on their organization, work ethic, and responsibility? What about late work? Here are a few thoughts on approaches to grading that are reasonable, practical, and measure mastery.

Author and educator Rick Wormeli loves to question traditional grading. He goes so far as to say, "Don't average the scores. The new score should replace the old one. Mastery is mastery. It shouldn't matter if it took the student one or three attempts to master the essentials." Whether you are thinking of assignments, homework, quizzes or exams, Wormeli makes an interesting point and challenges antiquated grading paradigms. Does it matter how many times they attempt to jump over a bar if they get to a place of understanding in the end? Isn't that the point of teaching and learning? Of course, a common counterargument to this philosophy is that students can game the system. If they intentionally fail (or don't really try) the first time in order to get exposure to the test content, they plan to ace it the second time around. This puts the onus on the teacher to create alternative tests, input and re-input different scores into the gradebook, and spend more time grading student work. But if your aim is student mastery, it is probably worth the time to create alternate assignments and assessments for students to have more opportunities to get there.

For the gradebook at large, consider how you determine your benchmarks or assignment values. Is your system reasonable? Could you reasonably explain it to a student, parent, or principal? I knew a teacher who used 10-point assignments early in the semester, 50-point assignments mid-way through, and 100-point assignments toward the end. It kept students motivated to turn in work throughout the semester as assignments grew in value, and it always gave students a chance to pass by the end. It also meant that early assignments were virtually meaningless in terms of impacting a final grade, but most students never caught on.

Also consider quantity of assignments and how often grades are updated. There is such a thing as too many assignments, or too few. In the digital age, students and parents have greater access to grades and assignments in real time. Frustration sets in when loads of assignments are entered each day or when assignments aren't entered for weeks. Keep it reasonable.

The point here is that it may be tricky to find the right balance. If you weight a gradebook too heavily toward assessments, then students who struggle with tests or demonstrating mastery will see their grades suffer, even if they do all the homework and classwork. If you weight a gradebook too heavily toward classwork and homework, students who master content and ace tests could fail your class.

Action Steps:

> **Ultimately, we all must make decisions about grading. Ask yourself this series of questions. As always, remember to work with your teams, colleagues, and administrators as you begin to answer these questions and establish or calibrate your gradebook policies.**

> **Does your grading policy place value on work ethic or mastery?**

> **Is it fair to students who struggle?**

- ➢ Are you entering too many assignments or too few?
- ➢ Are your policies reasonable?

Greg Noyes

The Struggle Is Real, Real Good, And Real Necessary

"People mainly fail because they fear failure." - Sebastian Thurn

"Life is not about how many times you fall down. It's about how many times you get back up." - Jaime Escalante

"Falling down is not a failure. Failure comes when you stay where you have fallen." - Socrates

2500 years after Socrates and many students still don't get it. In fact, in the digital age, our reluctance to embrace failure is a bigger problem than ever. The average college student has already spent 10,000 hours of their life playing video games, watched 20,000 hours of video content, and sent over 200,000 text messages. In these modern times we seem to want gratification immediately, we want to Google it, we need to watch it on YouTube, we have short attention spans, and we have 8-second filters. Teachers drop the ball for their students if they don't take the time to show them how to delay gratification, embrace patience, and properly contextualize failure. Show them that failing is a natural step while learning and use classroom strategies that match that philosophy. This is challenging as children today seem to be increasingly entitled, but it is not impossible.

There is no mutual exclusivity to praise and failure. Praise your students for their efforts, for sticking their necks out when they are unsure, for being vulnerable, and for being willing to fail. Teach your students that failure should be expected, that failure is natural, and that failure is always part of the learning process. This doctrine may be particularly difficult to engrain in students who have never really struggled in their academic pursuits and to whom learning has always come easy. As Doug Lemov puts it, "From the moment students arrived, the teachers worked to shape their perception of what it meant to make a mistake, pushing them to think of 'wrong' as a first, positive, and often critical step toward getting it" (Lemov, 2015).

To help them embrace this process, don't be in the habit of calling on a single student to answer a question, giving them an immediate reply, and moving on. That strategy guarantees that only a single individual put some thought into it. Instead, call on one student, then another, and then several more, without revealing whether any of their answers were right or wrong. This strategy guarantees that several students put thought into it, and likely several more as the rest anticipate being called on next. Oftentimes, the first answer is correct, but students conclude that you are looking for something more as you continue to survey the room. "Echoing" occurs this way as well, a strategy where many students repeat and hear the correct answer before moving on. Teacher wait-time allows more students to think, rationalize, rethink, analyze, or revisit the topic without you cutting to the chase.

Ultimately, there are plenty of reasons to help our students embrace failure. Struggling helps them in their educational careers and beyond. And there are also plenty of effective classroom strategies to match a failure-embracing philosophy. Help your learners to see that the struggle is real, that the struggle is good, and that the struggle is necessary.

Action Steps:

> **Discuss the three leading quotations with your students.**
> **Allow them to self-reflect as you ask them to apply it to their school experiences.**

Rigor Vs. Relevance
(Hint, Not Mutually Exclusive)

"I want to focus on relationships, relevance, and
rigor in that order." - Terie Engelbrecht

If the job of the teacher was simply to entertain, to be relatable, or to cover topics that students find interesting, some of us would be darn good at it. Students might not profit much in these scenarios. Likewise, if the job of the teacher was simply to push students, to create near-impossible challenges, or to set up endless hoops through which to jump, some of us would be darn good at that, too. Students might not learn or accomplish much in these scenarios either. The trick is to do both at the same time; to balance rigor and relevance.

In the world of education, rigor often refers to the complexity in which students are expected to operate. Rigor is found in learning experiences that are academically or intellectually challenging. Too little rigor and students are bored. Too much rigor and they are overwhelmed. Relevance, on the other hand, usually refers to the connection between what students are learning and what they care about. The more they care about what they are learning, the greater the relevance.

Simply put, learning should be fun, and it should profoundly matter to students. Learning should also be suitably challenging and complex. Part of the answer to this balancing act is found in how well you have built relationships with your students. If you tell them it will be fun and it matters, they are more likely to follow you if you have gained their trust. Part of the answer is also found in thoughtful lesson design that deliberately addresses rigor and relevance. Choose to make it fun. Articulate why it matters. Show them why they should care or how the exercise will impact their lives, both in the short term and in the long term. Yet another part of the answer is found in how students approach learning and how they perceive failure.

If they have been trained to seize the day and attack learning because they know it's important and they can see how it matters, they are more likely to view lessons with an eye for relevance. If they have been properly trained to consider failure as a necessary part of growth, they are less likely to give up when rigor is turned up. You control the dials for both rigor and relevance in your classroom. They need to be turned up in unison for optimal results. The teacher-student bond is the grease that loosens the dials. Form those bonds with your students and crank up the dials together.

Action Steps:

- ➢ **Reflect on rigor and relevance in your approach to teaching.**
- ➢ **Is learning fun in your class?**
- ➢ **Do students work hard?**
- ➢ **Do either of these dials need to be adjusted as you continue to build relationships with your students?**

Learning Modalities:
A Starting Place to Reach Them All

"If a child can't learn the way we teach, maybe we should teach them the way they learn." - Ignacio Estrada

A study of learning modalities or "learning styles" can be both insightful and transformative for educators. It can explain how we operate as instructors, and it can inform our teaching as we consider the learning modalities of our students. Different models have been proposed for learning styles, and I will be referencing from the following list of four: auditory, kinesthetic, tactile, and visual. In a nutshell, these models tell us that some students need to hear things in order to learn, some need to move their bodies while learning, some need to touch things, and others need to see things in order to remember them later.

Remember that a consideration of learning styles is separate from and complementary to differentiation in the classroom. It is also a bit different from a look at multiple intelligences, which also includes additional categories for being musical, interpersonal, logical, and so on. Although most students can access all four of the models listed above, many students have preferred learning styles, and some struggle with their weaker learning styles. Researchers conclude about learners:

- 25-30% are strongly visual (seeing)
- 25-30% are strongly auditory (hearing)
- less than 15% are tactile (touching)
- less than 10% are kinesthetic (moving)
- 25-30% are evenly mixed

As you are bound to work with students who prefer various learning modalities, here are a few generalities to keep in mind.

- Auditory learners tend to be analytical and task oriented. They love to know the answers to "What?" questions. They say, "Give me facts, please." They like to read or be read to, and they tend to verbally explain concepts or scenarios. Use shared inquiries and music as your secret weapons to get through to these learners.

- Kinesthetic learners can be dynamic and tend to see the big picture. They will often ask, "What if…" They model, demonstrate, or act things out. They say, "Let me show it to you, please." They are animated, outgoing, willing to take risks, and don't mind controlled chaos. Get them outside or at least moving around the room if you want to invigorate them.

- Tactile learners usually appeal to common sense and look for patterns in the details. They want to know, "How?" they say, "Let me try, please." They will translate things literally and are artistic and comfortable with clutter. Use manipulatives and hands-on materials whenever possible to help them grasp concepts.

- Visual learners will be imaginative and make things personally relatable. They need to ask, "Why?" They may want you to, "Give me a reason, please." They spell well, take notes, stay organized, and are detail oriented. Use charts, graphs, maps, and other visuals to help them learn in your class.

Action Steps:

➢ **Take into consideration the variety of learning modalities in your classroom as you teach.**

➢ **Make sure that you are actively appealing to how auditory, kinesthetic, tactile, and visual learners need to hear, move, touch, and see as they learn.**

Growth Mindset, In A Nutshell

"I don't believe in the gifted. If they have ganas [a winning attitude or desire], I can make them do it." - Jaime Escalante

"The definition of 'smart' simply means that you are ready to learn." - Freeman Hrabowski

"In a growth mindset, challenges are exiting rather than threatening. So rather than thinking, oh, I'm going to reveal my weaknesses, you say, wow, here's my chance to grow." - Carol S. Dweck

Along with many others, Stanford psychology professor Carol Dweck has popularized what is known as a *growth mindset* in recent years, contrasting it with a fixed mindset. For example, a fixed mindset sees failure as a limit of ability whereas a growth mindset sees failure as a growth opportunity. A fixed mindset means you stick to what you know, give up when frustrated, don't like a challenge, and believe you either get it or don't get it. A growth mindset means you try new things, turn up the effort when stymied, look for challenges, and believe you can learn anything you put your mind to.

Getting your students to view their academic pursuits with a growth mindset is largely dependent on how their teachers view their academic growth. Math hero Jaime Escalante puts it in simple terms, "If we expect kids to be losers, they will be losers; if we expect them to be winners, they will be winners. They rise, or fall, to the level of the expectations of those around them, especially their parents and their teachers." Freedom Writer legend Erin Gruwell is even more blunt, "It doesn't take a rocket scientist to figure out that if you tell kids they're stupid, directly or indirectly, sooner or later they start to believe it."

Being vulnerable, embracing growth opportunities, and facing constructive feedback can be a hard pill to swallow. No one likes to be exposed or hear about their weaknesses…at first. But once you and your students get past the fears, the real growth can happen. All students can succeed. If you begin to believe it, so will they.

Action Steps:

➢ For your students to succeed, you must first choose to believe it.

➢ Before you even meet them, decide that all your students can succeed.

➢ When there are challenges to the teaching and learning process, remind yourself that all your students can succeed. If you believe it, so will they.

Covenantal Vs. Contractual: Assuming Professional Best

*"Anyone else would have left you by now, but I'm sticking with you…
You're gunna show me the money." - Rod Tidwell (Jerry Maguire)*

*"If one a y'all says some silly…name, this whole class is gunna feel…
my…wrath." - Keegan-Michael Key's "Substitute Teacher" skit*

Covenantal and contractual agreements have existed for eons. In a covenantal agreement, both parties agree to keep up their end of the bargain. Think Noah, Abraham, Moses, or Jerry McGuire. A contractual agreement appeals to the letter of the law. Think education code, board policy, or teacher contracts. While it is absolutely necessary to have laws and rules to which we can appeal, it sure is nice to work in the realm of covenantal. Whether it is teachers working with teachers, or teachers working with administrators, a handshake should mean something, your word should mean something, and playing *gotcha* shouldn't be on our professional radar unless it must be.

It is best for students when everyone gets along, but realistically, relationships are bound to strain or have ups and downs. Some of us have experienced furloughs, walkouts, marches, and other types of labor disputes during our careers. Others of us haven't, and may not fully appreciate the relative labor peace we currently enjoy. What I am suggesting is that vertically (administrators above, or support staff below) or horizontally (other teachers), we assume the professional best of the people who work alongside us, the people who work for us, and the people for whom we work. I'm suggesting that we operate in the covenantal as a matter of principle until we are made to appeal to the contractual. In other words, until your hand is forced, assume the best of the professionals around you, just as you want the professional best assumed of you.

Working with your students is a completely different dynamic, but the covenantal/contractual dichotomy can function with them as well. The approach to dealing with students can similarly assume the best of them until they prove otherwise. Give your students the benefit of the doubt until they blow it. Anyone who has taught more than one hour knows that students will absolutely, unequivocally, and profoundly blow it. It's a certainty. They will miss assignments, forget homework, aggravate nerves, treat others unkindly, lie, cheat, steal, or worse. They will test your rules, break your rules, or even shatter your rules if you don't put your foot down. You can guarantee that you will have to get contractual on them and appeal to laws or rules eventually. But you don't have to come in piping hot like Mr. Garvey from the Key and Peele "Substitute Teacher" parody. There are more effective methods to address behavior and much better ways to build rapport with your students. Contrary to Mr. Garvey, your students don't always have to "feel…your…wrath."

Action Steps:

➤ **The next time a student misses a question, forgets homework, gets on your nerves, or breaks a rule, try operating in the covenantal realm to improve study habits or correct behavior.**

➤ **Talk with them. Work with them. Help them. Give them a chance until you must appeal to the contractual.**

What's Outside the Box?

"Those who do not think outside the box are easily contained." - Nicolas Manetta

"Instead of thinking outside the box, get rid of the box." - Deepak Chopra

Some of the most innovative classrooms are still just classrooms in the end, complete with floors, walls, desks, students, materials, and devices. As teachers, we tend to operate in educational boxes, both figuratively and literally. Yet all around the world, there are vastly different approaches to schooling, many of which are novel, innovative, research-based, inspiring, and barely recognizable to Western education.

For example, in Japan some schools are designed without classroom walls. Students have roof access, and are seen running around and playing for large portions of their instructional day. On average, they also walk an average of 4000 meters per day. In these schools, students achieve higher than their peers at neighboring schools (Block, 2017). Makoko Nigeria has 100 square foot floating schools that house 100 students at a time (Olisa, 2018). Orestad Gymnasium in Copenhagen Denmark is a giant glass cube, an alternative to traditional schooling that has high school students allied to solve real-world problems. The Brightworks School in San Francisco and the Blue School in New York let students get dirty, play with fire, disassemble appliances, and more. Innova Schools in Peru triple the Peruvian national average for math proficiency and have students spend half the day with tech-heavy online learning and half the day in (and out) of classrooms learning collaboratively (Weller, 2016).

Traveling to school can also be a noteworthy challenge. In fact, the commute to school can be a lesson in and of itself. Throughout the Himalayas, some children make a once-a-year journey to school that would put casual hikers to shame. Some students ride water buffalo to school in Myanmar (Shin, 2013). Along the Rio Negro in Colombia, students need to zip-line to get to school (Urbano, 2011). Regions of Indonesia feature students tight roping across rivers on steel cables or packing into small ferry boats as part of their daily commute to school (Kaushik, 2012).

In his book *Originals: How Nonconformists Move the World*, Adam Grant suggests that, "The greatest shapers don't stop at introducing originality into the world. They create cultures that unleash originality in others" (Grant, 2016). As shapers of minds and cultivators of classroom culture, teachers should aim to be original and creative in order to unleash originality and creativity in students. Perhaps it is time for you to step outside of the box, however small or brief your step may be. At the very least, share with your students some of the interesting, questionable, or amazing things happening in classrooms around the globe. Sometimes, systemic change that moves education outside of its boxes must happen high up the food chain, such as with the Department of Education or a state superintendent's office. Yet always remember that the teacher has their own powerful sphere of influence. Don't be afraid to occasionally step outside of some of your boxes as you teach.

Action Steps:

> Take a risk and do something outside the norm with your teaching.
> While you are at it, teach your students to take daily risks as they explore being original and creative.

Academic Freedom Vs. Common Lessons

"Free choice is one of the highest of all the
mental processes." - Mario Montessori

"Collaboration allows teachers to capture each other's
fund of collective intelligence." - Mike Schmoker

This issue can become divisive. Mr. Common says, "If we care about kids, we need to be on the same page with our lessons." "No, I need to be flexible if you want me to be good for my kids," says Ms. Freedom. "Common lessons are the best way to move all students along," says Common. "You sound like a Commie. I want my independence," says Freedom.

As primary grades focus heavily on reading and other skills, they tend to lean more toward common lessons. And as secondary grades ask students to apply their skills in specialized content areas, they tend to lean further toward academic freedom. There really are solid reasons to borrow a bit from the playbooks of both Mr. Common and Ms. Freedom. Like Mr. Common, you can more readily provide solid curriculum for all students if there are commonalities between teachers and their respective curricula. Like Ms. Freedom, you tap into boundless creative potential when you release teachers to design and create. Let's look at each school of thought and then consider some areas of compromise.

The argument for common lessons is rooted in Marzano's conclusions about a "guaranteed and viable curriculum" being the number one indicator for student achievement. Calibrating elements of curriculum is a powerful tool to expose all students to knowledge and skills. This could include pacing, grading and homework policies, lesson design, and common assessments within a grade level or department team. With commonalities in curriculum, teachers can compare apples-to-apples with their students' achievement. It's a shame when parents and students start to compare and request certain teachers in August in order to avoid others. Common lessons can help nip that problem in the bud.

There are plenty of reasons to exercise academic freedom as well. Not all teachers have the same pedagogical skillset or get excited about the same types of lessons. No two classrooms of students are the same either. Plus, asking teachers to be lock-step with others can sour the creative process. Teams of teachers with common lessons run the risk of falling into rote patterns. It is healthy for teachers, and beneficial for students, to be innovative and to have an open mind when it comes to their curriculum. Also, if student needs require pacing adjustment, teachers should have the flexibly to adjust pacing. Allowing teachers to have academic freedom unlocks worlds of potential.

One possible solution to bridge the gap between academic freedom and common lessons is a reasonable hybrid that synthesizes the best aspects of each. For instance, a team might agree on common pacing for when units begin and end, but the lesson designs are open for teachers to plan. Or a team agrees to share the more visible lessons, such as activities that students adore or parents appreciate. You don't want to face the annual question, "Why don't you do that cool rocket activity with your classes like Ms. Common does with hers?"

Another possible solution is to foster a culture where common planning is the norm. As lessons are conceived during collective planning time, often you will find that creative and dynamic lessons surface and are used by all. Freedom and commonality can become the same thing when teachers tap into their collective synergy. If a team of teachers allows for students to be the topic that drives conversation and curriculum decisions, good things will follow.

Another solution would be to let data drive the conversations. If teachers set aside egos and approach the table with an open mind, a genuine conversation about best-practices will emerge. When Mr. Freedom or Ms. Common consistently has students with higher test scores on shared assessments or state assessments, why wouldn't you want to figure out what they do and apply it to your own classroom? If you designed and implemented a lesson that is fun and effective with students, why wouldn't you want to share it?

Action Steps:

> ➤ **Whether you side with academic freedom or common lessons, decide to keep student learning a top priority.**

> ➤ **Consider hybrid approaches, plan with other teachers, and let data drive conversations about best-practices.**

A Fish Metaphor:
Don't Let Students Slip Past the Net

*"I am enough of a realist to understand that I can't
reach every child, but I am more of an optimist to get
up every morning and try." - Preston Morgan*

*"Just keep swimming. Just keep swimming.
Just keep swimming." - Dory (Finding Nemo)*

Fish can be a great metaphor for our students. They swim in schools, they can be raised in farms, there are big fish in little ponds, and there are fish that jump to bigger ponds. Fish an also slip through nets. Think about all the different types of students that need a little something extra to thrive, or even just to survive in our classrooms. We teach fish of all kinds; special needs, learning disabled, language learners, rich and poor, gifted and struggling. We have transient students, formerly homeschooled students, and students who find school culture unfamiliar. Using the fish analogy, consider the ways that you can assure that no guppies slip through your loving, educational net.

Watch for the fish out of water - A fish out of water has been plucked from its familiar environment and won't last for long. Students who speak English as a second language or come from outside the country can experience extreme culture shock and it can last for a long time. Be intentional about meeting their needs. Use appropriate strategies (G.L.A.D., English Language Development, etc.) to bridge language gaps for them. Go the extra mile for them. Show an interest in learning phrases in their native tongue. If they struggle with verbal communication, then they will certainly pick up on your body language, so show them that you care.

Watch for saltwater fish in freshwater - Students who come from a home culture that is vastly different from the school culture can stand out, and usually not in a good way. Sprinkle some salt into your lessons in order to help them acclimate to your freshwater classroom. Sing songs, introduce art, teach culturally relevant lessons, offer them choices, or provide opportunities for them to explore topics that are of interest to them.

Watch for fish thrown into new water - This extreme shock to the system is how pet goldfish meet their end, by the way. Students who enroll midyear or come from a completely different type of school setting (e.g. homeschool, private school, Non-Public School, group home, juvenile hall, bigger school, smaller school) may find our classrooms strange, foreign, or intimidating. Be intentional about breaking the ice, empathizing with their experiences, and offering added support. Get to know them early, connect them with peers, and check in with them often.

Action Steps:

➤ **Decide on a fish metaphor that fits best for a certain student in your classroom.**

➤ **Plan to support that student as prescribed above.**

Achievement Gaps:
Talking About the Elephants

"I want to see a skilled, qualified teacher who not only believes in the educability of the students that he or she is seeing, but has the tools and the wherewithal to bring that student to standard through instruction. I'm not as focused on whether that teacher is white, black, brown (or) multiracial." - Glenn Singleton

"Each parent sends you their best kid(s). It's not like they are keeping the good ones at home." - Donna Cherry

The Achievement Gap is not a single issue. There are many educational achievement gaps. On average, students from wealthy homes out-perform their underprivileged counterparts. Students from stable, two-parent homes out-perform students from homes with trauma. Students with learning disabilities are also out-performed. Let's face it, these gaps do exist, and schools have long been devising plans to address them. And in the age of COVID, school closures, and distance learning, many of these gaps are expected to get wider since resources and support at home are not equitable.

If there is a single, elephant-in-the-room, can't-ignore-it, punch-you-in-the-gut gap, it is the racial achievement gap. In schools and districts around the country, the story is much the same. Whether you look at grades, test scores, drop-out rates, or reading levels, vast gaps in achievement separate Asian, White, and Pacific Islanders from their Hispanic, Black, and Native classmates (Rowley, 2011). Minority groups deal with marginalization and are prevented from full participation in social, economic, and political life in ways that privileged groups can never fully appreciate. This is often the case in schools as well.

Glen Singleton's *Courageous Conversations about Race* is a fabulous viewpoint from which to begin the conversation about this racial achievement gap. In it, he highlights necessary conditions to begin the conversation. These include establishing immediate racial context, keeping the conversational spotlight on race, keeping everyone at the table, defining race as a social construct, and recognizing that success is often unfairly linked with adaptation to white culture. Growth mindset comes into play here as well. TED Talker Eric Mahmoud refers to a "belief gap" as the real culprit behind the achievement gap. If we don't believe our students are capable, they won't believe it either and the status quo will persist (Easley, 2016).

My teaching career debuted in a beautifully diverse middle school in South Sacramento. By certain measures, it was considered the most diverse zip code in America. At one point, our school was almost exactly 25% Black, 25% Hispanic, 25% Asian, and 25% "everything else." These demographic quadrants included subcategories as well: Salvadorian, Guatemalan, Mexican, Filipino, Marshallese, Fijian, Tongan, Samoan, Hmong, Mien, Laotian, Cambodian, Russian, Ukrainian, Romanian. Parent information went home in at least 12 languages. Our challenges were unique, but so were our opportunities. I recall school leadership deciding to take a unique approach to addressing the achievement gap by inviting large groups of students to assembly talks. Hispanic, Black, White, and Asian student leaders, who were only middle schoolers themselves, introduced the achievement gap head on, leading their peers through slideshows, graphics, and discussions.

At least six things happened. First, by nature of the talks, the process was an exercise in racial reconciliation. Second, our previously uninformed students were now informed about the achievement gap. Third, many of our students developed a healthy balance of being both unsatisfied and motivated when it came to addressing the gaps. Fourth, our students began to see that their efforts would mean something, that they represented not only themselves and their families, but their racial demographic and their school. Fifth, the teaching staff grew bolder and more comfortable in addressing these issues in the classroom. Sixth, scores went up dramatically that year as a result of our students and teachers being better informed, unsatisfied with past results, and motivated to make changes.

Don't ignore the racial achievement gap or any of the other achievement gaps. Admittedly, conversing with students, parents, or staff directly about achievement gaps in assemblies, classrooms, or individually can be uncomfortable. But they are courageous and necessary conversations if anything is to change.

Action Steps:

- ➤ **Reflect on your own views about achievement gaps.**
- ➤ **What are some causes that you believe are to blame?**
- ➤ **What are some solutions that you have seen work or are willing to try?**
- ➤ **For you personally, or for your staff collectively, is there also a belief gap that might first need to be reconciled before focusing on closing any achievement gaps?**

Instructional Rounds:
Sharpening Best Practices

"Is anyone wise to learn by the experience of others?" - Voltaire

Players scout their rivals. Authors read the books of others. Directors watch films that aren't their own. And teachers watch others teach. Teachers often do this to inform their instruction or sharpen their craft. In order to improve learning on a larger scale, teachers and teacher leaders watch classroom instruction on a formal, wider scope as well. These organized walkthroughs are popularly known as "learning walks" or "instructional rounds."

A title borrowed from "grand rounds" practiced in medical school, instructional rounds (IR) is just a fancy title for systematic sessions of purposeful classroom walkthroughs. Traditionally, the purpose of IR is to discern the causes of previously identified issues within the school, to identify what is happening in classrooms, and to give a school direction with respect to potential outcomes. The subject of instructional rounds might be open-ended, or might include any number of specific elements in the classroom, such as: learning objectives, gradual release, differentiation, modeling, wait-time, rigor, critical thinking, checking for understanding, student engagement, classroom routines, structured student interaction, pacing, or transitions.

IR can happen districtwide, schoolwide, department-wide, or even between a few individual teachers. And although IR is conventionally district driven, grassroots IR occurs as well. In fact, when teachers are motivated to do IR, they are usually highly motivated to help their students and promote positive changes within their respective spheres of influence. I have been part of IR at all levels, from districtwide initiatives down to just a few teachers. I have seen IR that was largely unsuccessful and rejected by staff, and I have been part of IR that was tremendously successful and transformative. If you are looking to pioneer or partake in IR at your site, consider these points of suggestion.

First, if you want teacher buy-in, IR cannot and should not be evaluative. I loved hearing the motto "look down, not up" as a guideline. This suggests that the subject of IR is what students are asked to do and how they respond as opposed to a focus on the teacher's instruction. I was once the subject of visiting IR teams that gave me a score of "zero" when measuring a posted learning objective. Little did they know that our class covered it on the slideshow before the IR team walked in. I knew it wasn't evaluative, but it still didn't feel good to get a zero. Many of my colleagues were similarly turned off by that part of the process and the IR efforts fell flat.

Second, it is important to be realistic with IR goals. Don't focus on all 13 examples listed above. Choose one or two, three at the most. It would be overwhelming for both the observers and the observed if a long checklist of items was part of the process. In the case of IR, depth is better than breadth. Trying to be the jack of all trades makes you master of none. Using a standardized form to take notes also assures common points of focus for observers. Keep it simple, focused, and realistic.

Third, break it up in order to put it back together. Sending different teams to watch entire 30-minute or 60-minute isolated lessons is not ideal for the IR process. If teams of observers rotate every 10-15 minutes to see different parts of the same lessons, you not only get diverse insights about the same classroom, but teams also must collaborate afterward and piece it back together. If you send different teams to rotate between parts of lessons in different classes, they are each able to see different parts of same lessons.

Fourth, be intentional about what to do next. The follow-up discussion is arguably as valuable as the observations themselves. Some observers might have completely different takeaways from the same lesson. Some might have seen the opening of the lesson while others saw the closure. Set aside time to discuss what you observed. And be sure to have a process of sharing your findings with the teachers that were observed as well.

Action Steps:

- ➤ With the purpose being to improve your teaching and help students, pioneer or participate in instructional rounds at your site.
- ➤ Make sure it is non-evaluative, has realistic goals, encourages collaboration, and has next steps in mind.

Draw Inspiration from History's Educational Champions

"All hail the underdogs, all hail the new kids, all hail the outlaws, Spielbergs and Kubricks." - X Ambassadors

"You will never influence the world by being just like it." - Kay Marshal

As I considered my classroom design strategy, I decided to put pictures of all sorts of famous and not-so-famous people on the walls. To make the cut, a person had to be special, or at least have some style. I considered all fields, from musicians and actors to inventors and world leaders. These included celebrities like Hugh Jackman, Jimmy Fallon, and Audrey Hepburn, artists like Kirk Franklin, Woody Guthrie, and U2, champions like Roger Federer, Serena Williams, and Michael Phelps, fictional characters like Quicksilver, Batman, and the cast of The Walking Dead, as well as pioneers like Emilia Earhart, Neil Armstrong, and Stanley Kubrick. And seeing as I was in a place of teaching and learning, I made sure to make room for my educational heroes as well.

Across eras, languages, countries and continents, education has boomed and bellowed. Certain groups have been denied access to education, in some places, education has found breakthroughs, and in other places people are still fighting for educational rights. The story of education is long, inspiring, and ongoing. There are enough educational trailblazers to fill a library full of books. Take a moment to consider and be inspired by a few of them.

Aristotle established the Lyceum to help further philosophy and science. His teacher Plato had previously founded the Academy with a similar purpose. Prior to that, Plato's teacher Socrates routinely challenged the Sophists, the self-appointed philosophical authorities of Athens. Centuries later, Jesus similarly challenged the Pharisees and Sadducees, teaching and fraternizing with the poor, with women, and with sinners. Martin Luther translated the Bible into the German vernacular, releasing knowledge from papal control and giving scriptural access to commoners. Sojourner Truth and Harriet Tubman both escaped slavery to become activists fighting for black rights, women's rights, and educational rights. Former slave Booker T. Washington focused specifically on education for formerly enslaved African Americans. Malala Yousafzai suffered and survived a bullet in the head for demanding access to education for women in the Arab world. They all pushed limits. They all consciously enraged authorities. They all questioned status quos. They all loved teaching and learning. They all blazed trails. As a classroom teacher, every day be inspired by these visionaries and allow your students to be, too.

Action Steps:

> **Put a picture of your favorite educational leader on the wall and tell your students why they are so heroic.**

> **Better yet, post pictures of dozens of them and make a point to explain the circumstances, courage, and heroism for each of them throughout the course of the school year.**

Students Teaching *You?*
Slow to Speak, Quick to Listen

"When one teaches, two learn." - Robert Heinein

"If you want to be creative, stay in part a child, with the creativity and invention that characterizes children before they are deformed by adult society." - Jean Piaget

Whether you teach five-year-olds or eighteen-year-olds, you can learn incredible things from your students if you are willing to listen. Reflect on these methods closing your mouth and opening your ears.

Be aware of how much you talk in class. Certain studies have concluded that students need a processing period between teacher talk time. The terms "10:2 ratio," "5-1" and "chunk and chew" refer to the need for student process time (e.g. teacher talks for ten minutes, then students talk for two minutes). This ratio becomes even more crucial with younger learners who can't listen to you talk for more than a few minutes at a time. Stop talking and let them digest the information.

Circulate the room and listen to the conversations that are taking place. Gathering feedback from your students allows you to strategically adjust instruction as necessary. You may identify a need to reteach a concept, to correct common errors in their thinking, to move on as planned, or to increase the pace of instruction. You won't always know where to go or what to do if you don't listen to your students first.

Give your students a formal survey about your teaching. You might do it midyear and look to adjust in January. You might do it in June and reflect over the summer. At some point, ask them what they think of you. This undoubtedly puts you in a place of vulnerability, yet asking for specific feedback about your class, your lessons, or about your work as a teacher can be profoundly insightful. Occasionally, you might get feedback that stings, but sometimes we need our blemishes exposed in order to develop and grow as educators. Extra Credit assignment: If you really buy into this approach, give your parents a survey about your class as well.

Action Steps:

> ➢ **It is difficult to listen if you don't stop talking.**
>
> ➢ **Be aware of how much you talk to your students.**
>
> ➢ **Go around the room and listen to your students in order to guide instructional decisions.**
>
> ➢ **Create a mid-year or end-of-year survey in order to gather information from your students that will help to inform your teaching.**

Perfect Teachers Don't Have Perfect Students

"Of all the hard jobs around, one of the hardest is
being a good teacher." - Maggie Gallegher

There is a well-known parenting adage that goes something like, "Perfect parents don't have perfect children, but they know what to do when they aren't perfect." Running a classroom full of students has its parallels with running a household with your own children. In the classroom, you are their surrogate parent for much of the day, the week, and the year. Like it or not, teachers are a bit like substitute parents when they are on the job. In a very real way, the teacher is a surrogate parent for large chunks of a child's waking hours. *In loco parentis* (in place of a parent) is a reference to the legal responsibility that schools assume and is commonly found in state education codes.

Your students will misbehave in your classroom. You can bet on it. When they do, it doesn't mean you are a bad teacher, but it does leave you with some choices to make to address the misbehavior. The importance of consistency and accountability here cannot be overstated. In a general sense, let students know where your lines are, and hold them accountable by following through with a reasonable response when they cross those lines.

Some teachers think that sending a student to the office on referral reflects poorly on their classroom management. On the contrary, it is vital to keep counselors or administrators in the loop with student concerns. Ask for guidance or support well in advance of your breaking point. And unless a student incident is egregious, you don't want the first parent contact to come from the office, you want it to come from you. The moment you outsource your discipline problems is the moment you give up a certain level of control and accountability with your students. Not to mention, you as the classroom teacher have the unique power to practice restorative justice with your students (e.g. a focus reconciliation between the offender and the offended, whether that is the teacher or other students).

For students who misbehave, communicate with home regularly (even when things are going well). You might be the first person to tell them their little angel is imperfect, especially in primary grades. But it is important to communicate honestly and purposefully. It is extremely unfortunate when a parent gets the first phone call in March that goes something like, "He was horrible today and come to think of it, he's pretty much been like this all year." Home support is indispensable, so give parents a chance to help by holding their children accountable at home as well. Just as perfect parents don't have perfect children, perfect teachers don't have perfect students. But if you know what to do and how to respond when they make mistakes, you are approaching greatness.

Action Steps:

➢ **First, acknowledge that your students aren't perfect, and that is not a reflection on you or your classroom management.**

➢ **Second, apply consistency, accountability, restoration, and honest communication to appropriately respond, correct, and redirect.**

Hey Students, Free Education Is A Recent Phenomenon

*"If ever there was a cause worthy to be upheld by all
the toil and sacrifice that the human heart can endure,
it is the cause of education." - Horace Mann*

Do your students realize what a privilege it is to be sitting in their desks right now? Yes, it is a privilege! Historically speaking, school was only for the privileged few. In Medieval Europe for example, most peasants were illiterate and couldn't afford school. In the pre-Civil War South, slaves were forbidden from learning and often severely beaten for trying to read books at night. The free public education that we all enjoy in this country is an historically rare phenomenon that many of us take for granted. What a privilege it is to be at school right now!

America is often called The Land of Opportunity. Not only have millions of immigrants come here to escape religious persecution, oppressive governments or violence, but also to live a better life. In America, school is free for children, college can be very affordable, and jobs pay much more than in other countries. For these reasons, hundreds of thousands flood into the states each year. Are your students capitalizing on the fact that they live in this land of Opportunity?

In many countries, education is not free. In some third world countries, schooling for just one child could cost half of a family's income. As a result, many families can't afford to send any of their children to school. Would the parents of your students see them through school if it cost half of their income? If they could only afford to put one of their children through school, which child would have the best chance at success? Tough call. Fortunately, the students and families that we serve do not have to make such decisions since school is free for at least thirteen years: kindergarten through twelfth grade, and then can be reasonably affordable after that.

To date, education is still not allowed everywhere. In locations throughout the Arab world for instance, schooling is disallowed for parts of the population, especially women. Just ask Malala Yousafzai, who survived a bullet for trying to go to school then and went on to be the youngest winner of the Nobel Peace Prize in 2014. The free public education that we all enjoy in the United States is a globally rare phenomenon that many students take for granted. Help your students maintain an attitude of gratitude.

Action Steps:

> **With the intention of promoting an attitude of gratitude, share some of this information with your students.**

Learning Communities: Going Beyond Weekly Meetings

"A professional learning community is a collaboration of teachers, administrators, parents, and students who work together to seek out the best practices, test them in the classroom, continuously improve processes, and focus on results." - Rick DuFour

Though the title can quickly grow esoteric, Professional Learning Communities (PLCs) have existed for ages. Also known as critical friends, collaboration communities, or learning groups, PLCs are at the most basic level a group of professionals that come together to learn. More developed PLCs are groups of educators that regularly meet, share, and collaborate to improve teaching and learning. Teachers are usually a main PLC staple, but PLCs can and should go beyond teachers as well. PLCs are commonly found to exist as entire faculty teams or school site teams, but also can apply to smaller groups such as leadership teams, cross-curricular teams, department teams, or grade level teams in and around school sites.

Many groups in schools and districts around the country are teamed by necessity or obligation, and do not resemble high-functioning PLCs. Remember that teaching isn't meant to be a solo endeavor. If you need help, you have capable professionals around you. If you are such a prodigy by yourself, do the rest of your colleagues a favor and humbly work with them to make everyone better. We expect our students to practice 21st century skills, which include collaboration and communication. As educators, we should be the most exemplary and tangible model of collaboration for our students. Whether teaching comes easy to you or not, don't be on an island. Here are some things you could be doing to either contribute to an already functioning PLC or to help establish a genuine PLC.

Find common planning time. Many school schedules have built common planning time into the calendar. Take advantage of this and work with your peers.

Use common assessments. Comparing students and scores is a useful starting point by which to candidly discuss best practices in the classroom.

Watch each other teach. This is a wonderful habit to establish, even for veterans. Observing one another teach leads to productive and fruitful discussions, as well as novel ideas and lesson enhancement.

Maintain a personal growth mindset while promoting a collective growth mindset within the PLC. Even the best of us can get better, particularly when we work together.

Action Steps:

➢ **Promote professional learning communities within your spheres of influence by planning with other teachers, watching others teach, inviting others to watch you teach, modeling a growth mindset, and involving all stakeholders in the teaching and learning process.**

College-Bound?
Not Everyone Is Going and That's Okay

"The mission of schools today is to prepare all students to work at jobs that do not yet exist, creating ideas and solutions for products and problems that have not yet been identified, using technologies that have not yet been invented." - Linda Darling-Hammond (The Flat World and Education)

Whether you teach young kiddos just learning about the idea of college or instruct teens who are actively applying to colleges, you ought to be talking about school beyond the twelfth grade and you ought to be giving them accurate information as well. It is a noble goal to want all our learners to pursue bachelor's degrees or higher, but not all will go down that road. After receiving a high school diploma, there are many ways for our students to continue priming for a successful career or fulfilling life, and not all of them include college. It is almost sacrilegious for some educators to concede this point, but it's actually acceptable for students to do something other than go straight to college. Here are a few non-traditional educational pathways to discuss with your young scholars, some of which require some college, some of which require none at all.

Separate from conventional colleges and universities, trade schools and vocational schools prepare students for specific hands-on careers such as nursing, carpentry, or for becoming a technician or other specialist. More than 50% of all manufacturing jobs require post-secondary degrees or certificates. Auto mechanics, for example, need college-level reading, algebra and geometry skills to read factory manuals and analyze diagnostic data on the vehicles they are servicing. Likewise, all five branches of the military require new recruits to have high school diplomas and encourage additional training as well. Even fast food restaurants and retail stores want workers who at least have high school diplomas. In some cases, these companies not only encourage more education for their employees, they will provide it or pay for it.

Help your students to look further down the road and consider their educational future and professional careers. If they hear from teachers each year that they will continue with affordable schooling after high school, the idea will eventually stick. They will walk in that paths we set before them. Help your students to play it safe and play it smart. Help them to plan for college after high school. And if that is not feasible, expose them to the over-abundance of other routes that they may take before entering the workforce.

Action Steps:

> ➢ **Plan an age-appropriate and calculated discussion with your students about college and career readiness.**

Making Students Better, Not Bitter

*"Supervision should be used as a formative way to give
feedback to teachers to support their growth." - Paul Mielke*

A few years ago, Wisconsin natives Paul Mielke and Tony Frontier wrote a powerful book titled, *Making Teachers Better, Not Bitter, Balancing Evaluation, Supervision, and Reflection for Professional Growth.* It was named such because a teacher uttered a similar phrase to Mielke during a recent evaluation, and he knew something had to change. In the book, the pair emphasizes the need not just to measure teachers for measurement's sake, but to help them grow. Frontier and Mielke make a threefold case for: evaluation of teachers that is genuine, supervision of teachers that empowers, and encouragement of teachers to meaningfully and purposefully reflect on their practice.

As with most literature about teachers, the wisdom here can and should be applied to the classroom as well. Take each of their three points in turn. First, we ought to be evaluating our *students* genuinely. Our students should learn to rely on the conclusions and feedback from teachers regarding their performance, trusting that the teacher takes the time to consider their performance as an individual student, knowing that the teacher will provide direction for growth.

Second, we ought to be present with our *students*, supervising them in a way that focuses and empowers. Just like a coach on the sidelines, we need to offer constant feedback, keeping them on track and excited for future challenges in the course of their learning. Third, we ought to set aside daily time for *students* to reflect on their learning. Teachers establish the parameters in order to provide context and meaning, and then they can ask students to contemplate their performance, their understanding, or their growth. Mielke and Frontier propose that teachers are at their best when they self-supervise, self-evaluate, and self-reflect. There is no reason to think this isn't also true of our students.

Just as with administrators and teachers working together, the relationship between a teacher and a student should be much more about measuring growth than about evaluation. Yes, we still need to evaluate our students, but not as an end goal. We don't measure in order to separate the wheat from the chaff. We don't evaluate to reward and punish with corresponding letter grades. Instead, be present with your students as you consistently evaluate their progress, knowledge, and skills.

Action Steps:

- ➢ **Make your students better, not bitter.**
- ➢ **Consider your classroom as a place that focuses student efforts and empowers them to reach higher and be part of the process.**
- ➢ **Provide intentional opportunities for student reflection.**

A Sensible Perspective on High Stakes Testing

"Sometimes the most brilliant and intelligent minds do not shine in standardized tests because they do not have standardized minds." - Diane Ravitch

Valuable assessment tool. Unnecessary use of instructional time. Measuring stick. Break from instruction. Time to perform. Necessary evil. Opinions on standardized testing are strong and varied. I proctored tests as a classroom teacher and have also directed testing sitewide at my school. Consider again the thesis-antithesis-synthesis model (an idea, an opposing idea, and a practical blend of the two ideas) as applied to standardized testing.

First consider this *thesis* supporting the merits of standardized testing - Student achievement is of the upmost importance, and we ought to use standardized means by which to measure student achievement. We need a way to justifiably compare students and ensure that we are keeping students, teachers, schools, districts, and states accountable.

Consider the *antithesis*, challenging the usefulness of standardized testing - Testing is not a good use of instructional time, driving educators to "teach to the test" or worse. Some teachers might be pressed to resist collaboration or cheat, especially if pay or other benefits are tied to student test scores. Standardized testing brings unnecessary stress to students and teachers.

Now consider a *synthesis* in which these two ideas could sensibly be blended together - Make standardized testing an extension of instruction, not a break from it. Prepare students throughout the year by giving them opportunities to practice the skills they will need to apply on standardized assessments. Work to change the culture of standardized testing from high-stakes, stressful, and traumatic to exciting, useful, and informative.

Student performance drives instruction, and instruction prepares students to perform.

In his book *Ethical Leadership,* Robert Starratt makes the case that the role of teachers and leaders in the pressure-cooker of high-stakes testing is deeply moral. Leaders struggle to do the right thing for students and teachers as they are pressured and punished by state-mandated tests. Starratt reminds leaders that the answer lies in being proactively *responsible,* professionally *authentic,* and resolutely *present* (Starratt, 2004). One way I saw this manifest was via a "state testing fantasy league." Teachers drafted students who they believed would improve from the previous year. The league made a world of difference as scores went up and stress went down. Students will perform if for no other reason than they know who you are, and they like you.

After reading this, you probably still have strong opinions on testing. At the very least, have some level of awareness and a new appreciation for both sides of the standardized testing debate. Recent changes in some approaches to testing are positive steps. Some states have distanced themselves from knowledge-based assessments (content-based multiple choice) and have moved toward skill based-assessments (performance tasks and analysis). Getting rid of testing completely would create an accountability chasm. The drive to place more performance pressure on teachers and students has and will be subject to the law of diminishing return. The answer may always be somewhere in between. And a key to shaping and refining standardized assessments into something worthwhile will be found in our collective mindset as educators.

Action Steps:

➢ **Do you have strong opinions on standardized testing?**

➢ **Acknowledge that there are valid arguments to support the viewpoints of those who disagree with you.**

➢ Apply Starratt's guidance for leaders by being responsible, authentic, and present during testing season, as well as during ongoing discussions regarding testing.

I Think I Got This Teaching Thing Down, Now What?

"Each of us, from those early in our careers to those more seasoned, has room to grow and improve." - H. Richard Milner IV

What a wonderful feeling to go into a school year with a newfound confidence in your teaching abilities. For many teachers, this happens around year three. In year one, there can be a great deal of learning things the hard way, of beg, borrow, and steal, of late nights and weekends planning, and of leaning on others for resources, lesson plans, and direction. This is not to mention the fact that first year teachers also get sick about half a dozen times from August to May. Tremendous growth tends to occur by year two as teachers approach curriculum and classroom management with fresh perspective. Second year teachers are still finding their identity, adjusting lessons, trying new things, and enjoying successes in the classroom with regularity. By year three, many teachers find themselves in an "I got this" state of mind. This may also happen years later, but when a teacher finally arrives at "I got this," it comes with a feeling of relief and empowerment. So, you're a pro. Now what? Don't worry, you still have plenty of options in terms of where to apply your professional energies.

The first and most obvious option is to continue to find ways to improve each year. Your students are always changing, so you had better plan to adapt as well. Even the most effective lessons need to be revisited and reevaluated with relevance and rigor in mind. Second, find your niche at school or switch to a new niche if it is time to move on. There are so many things happening each year, including: book fairs, clubs, sports, assemblies, field trips, yearbooks, student newspapers, or daily bulletins. Be the *go-to person* for something at your school site.

Third, devote some time to grant writing. There are bountiful monies available for your school and your classroom if you take the time to do a little light research. Every teacher can receive educational grants. You don't have to necessarily be a good writer; you just have to have a need and find a grant that matches.

A fourth option is to look for opportunities to take on a formal leadership role. All teachers have leadership qualities as they lead students each day. Look for opportunities to lead your department, grade level, to be a union representative, or to participate in curriculum steering.

Even if you aren't a natural leader, at the very least, pay it forward with your colleagues by pouring your expertise and energies into making the people around you better. Be the one that the principal can trust to come alongside a new or struggling teacher, or to be the voice of reason during difficult conversations. That moment when you get comfortable with your teaching is a satisfying feeling. But beware, *comfortable* can morph into *complacent*, and *complacent* is just a few steps away from *lazy* or *ineffective*.

Action Steps:

- ➤ **By all means, celebrate your successes and enjoy the satisfaction of becoming very good at your craft.**
- ➤ **But also, be on the lookout for what's next.**
- ➤ **Consider your legacy.**
- ➤ **Get better, find your place, lead or pour into those around you.**

Get Up, Get Out, Go See the World

*"The world is a book, and those who do not travel
read only a page." - Saint Augustine*

*"The world is a university and everyone is a teacher. Make sure
when you wake up in the morning you go to school." - T.D. Jakes*

Whether to relax, escape, celebrate, expand your knowledge, lose yourself, or find yourself, most people love to travel. And people with time and money tend to travel often. Teaching is a profession that allows for such travel, thanks to a fair middle-class income and an enviable schedule that gives teachers every weekend, holiday, and summer off. Unlike many professions, teachers are able to purposefully relate travel to their profession. What you learn from your journeys often finds its way back into your classroom. In short, people like traveling, teachers can have the time, the means, and a unique profession-driven reason to do it.

Save, plan, go. And then bring your experiences back with you to inform your teaching. Do something wild, do something relaxing, or mingle the two. Backpack in Europe. Explore Rio, Sydney, or Cairo. Hike Machu Picchu, Mount Fuji, or Mount Kilimanjaro. Road trip to national landmarks. Go to the nearby coast or mountains. Pack up some friends, the kids, the spouse, or the dogs. Just get going.

Sometimes, traveling for work instead of pleasure can do the job as well. Teaching abroad for a season, going on a mission trip, working with an organization like Teach for America, or visiting a professional development or conference can provide insight to education, to other cultures, and to different teaching approaches. Save, plan, go. The rest and relaxation, the irreplaceable memories, and the newfound insights can and will make you a better teacher.

Action Steps:

- ➢ Budget time and resources to get up, get out, and go see something new. Plan to do this during the next available break from work.

- ➢ If circumstances don't allow for this, then at the very least, go on a day trip to some place new or some place you haven't visited in a long while.

Students' Work: Tie It Up with A Proverbial Bow

"How lucky I am to have something that makes saying goodbye so hard." - Winnie the Pooh

It was a pet peeve of mine to see students fill the trash cans with schoolwork on the last day of school. I pleaded with them, "Let your parents see it first!" or "At least take it home and throw it away there!" That collection of work meant something to me, and I wanted it to mean something to my students as well. In some ways, it represented a year's worth of our blood, sweat, and tears as we learned and created together. Surely it deserved better than to be destined for the dumpster. At a certain age (usually around middle school) the decision about whether to keep or scrap the schoolwork falls less on the parent and more on the student. In either case, the teacher can take steps to ensure that at least some of that meaningful work will be preserved.

Frame and contextualize the work for your students. Remind them, "You have worked extremely hard this year. This represents a year of effort. We can be proud of this." You could even have a cover page of sorts that says something to the effect of, "My third-grade year, in a nutshell." In jest, remind them that they can show it off to their grandkids one day. I had students who ran into me years later and told me verbatim, "Mr. Noyes, I still have all the work from your class! I just couldn't throw it away." The learning in my class had enormous value to them. What a compliment that was.

Have the foresight to organize (or direct them to organize) their work in a meaningful way before Open House or by the end of the year, whenever you hand it over to them. If you pass back work sporadically, students usually aren't willing or able to tie it up with a proverbial bow. Don't be surprised if it is lost or thrown away. Consider having students use one binder with all major work from each unit by the end of school. Wait to pass back all major activities at spring Open House. Perhaps you have a day where you collectively separate the wheat from the chaff, designating a small folder or binder as the "keepers." Organize the work in such a way that they would think twice before getting rid of it. Make it pretty. Make it a work of art. Make it matter.

Communicate to your students a rule about throwing work away. If you have established any sort of bonds with your students, they will have pause when you tell them it matters to you. Give them some guidelines. Or better still, give them choices. Maybe you ask students to choose from one of the following options: store your work away for safe keeping, take pictures of your work before throwing it away, show it off to a parent or a sibling before throwing it away.

If you want your trash cans to be free of students' hard work at the end of the school year, talk to them about it. If you think the journey you all took together had meaning, help them organize it in a meaningful way. If you want the work to matter to them, let them know how much it matters to you.

Action Steps:

> ➤ **Adjust your end-of-year practices with respect to "putting a bow" on student work or find a new way to encourage your students to reflect and place value on their year of learning.**

The Send-Off:
This Is the Greatest Profession on Earth

"Teacher? I prefer the term 'educational Rockstar'." – a teacher meme

"Those who can't do, teach." "Those who can't teach, teach P.E."
"Those that can't teach P.E. become administrators." Ever heard
any of those ones before? It's nonsensical and insulting. If it
were true, then anyone could do it. And we know with certainty
that not everyone can do it. I like this line instead, "Those who
can't teach try to pass laws about how to evaluate teachers."

Teachers have the highest of callings and have been an invaluable part of every culture throughout history. For that matter, P.E. teachers and administrators have too. Teachers are part of a benevolent global force that must adapt to an ever-changing world with ever-changing students. New trends drive new teaching and content standards. New technology allows for new approaches to teaching and learning. New job fields necessitate new courses and curricula. New ideas mean new frontiers. New civic leaders have new agendas. New world developments create new challenges. New gurus propose new paradigms. All these factors make our classrooms and the teaching profession incomparably dynamic.

Precious few other professions are forced to adapt so rapidly. Ask a handful of veterans about the major differences in education now compared to their first year of teaching, and then listen to their variety of answers. This is an exhilarating, challenging, and rewarding profession that can bring out the best of anyone and invites teachers to be life-long learners. When you get to a place where you think to yourself, "I think I'm getting the hang of this," don't coast. Don't be the teacher who goes beyond their expiration date and is only sticking around for the paycheck. Press on to improve. There is nothing more inspiring than a rock-star veteran teacher who continues to set personal improvement goals and tenaciously pursues them. When they retire, people say, "I'm happy for them, but what big shoes to fill. They were at the top of their game." That's the way to go out.

Teachers have the power to exponentially impact lives. You have the stage with eyes wide open and minds ready to soak up whatever you say or do. You may have thousands of students throughout your career. Many of them may become teachers themselves and impact thousands more because of you. Go for it and press on until the time comes to hang it up. Follow the countless educators that came before you to prove this as the most noble of callings. Do your part to continue the legacy of the teaching business. After all, being a teacher is the greatest profession on Earth.

Action Steps:

> ➤ **Think of a colleague that is just beginning their career, approaching retirement, or may be struggling; professionally, personally, or otherwise. Share this final excerpt with them by way of encouragement.**

References

Block, India (2017). Tokyo kindergarten by Tezuka Architects lets children run free on the roof. Dezeen. Retrieved from: https://www.dezeen.com/2017/10/02/fuji-kindergarten-tokyo-tezuka-architects-oval-roof-deck-playground/

Bonwell, C., & Eison, J. (1991). Active learning: Creating excitement in the classroom (ASHE-ERIC Higher Education Report No. 1). Washington, DC: George Washington University. Abstract online at http://www.ed.gov/databases/ERIC_Digests/ed340272.html

Bonwell, C., & Eison, J. (1993, January). Recent works on using active learning strategies across the disciplines. Unpublished manuscript. ERIC Document Reproduction Service No. ED 364 135.

Bornstein, M.H. 2012. "Caregiver Responsiveness and Child Development and Learning: From Theory to Research to Practice." In *Infant/Toddler Caregiving: A Guide to Cognitive Development and Learning*, ed. P.L. Mangione, 2nd ed. Sacramento: California Department of Education.

Violence Prevention. CDC. https://www.cdc.gov/violenceprevention/childabuseandneglect/acestudy/aboutace.html

Easley II, Jacob, & Tulowitzki, Pierre (2016). Educational Accountability: International perspectives on challenges and possibilities for school leadership. Routledge, NY, p36.

Fredricks, J. A. (2014). Eight Myths of Student Disengagement: Creating Classrooms of Deep Learning. Los Angeles: Corwin.

Froebel, Friedrich (2015). Frobelweb.org. Retrieved from: Froebelweb.org

Fullan, Michael. (2011). The Six Secrets of Change. Hoboken, NJ: Jossey-Bass.

Graesser, A., & Person, N. K. (1994). Question asking during tutoring. *American Educational Research Journal*, 31, 104-137.

Harvard Health Letter (2010, July). *A prescription for better health:go alfresco*. Retrieved from https://www.health.harvard.edu/newsletter_article/a-prescription-for-better-health-go-alfresco

Hattie, John (2015). Hattie Ranking: 252 Influences And Effect Sizes Related To Student Achievement. Visible Learning. Retrieved from: https://visible-learning.org/hattie-ranking-influences-effect-sizes-learning-achievement/

Kaushik (2012). Kids Risking Their Lives to Reach School. Amusing Planet. Retrieved from: https://www.amusingplanet.com/2013/03/kids-risking-their-lives-to-reach-school.html

Könings KD, Brand-Gruwel S, van Merriënboer JJG. (2010). An approach to participatory instructional design in secondary education: an exploratory study. Educ Res.; 52(1):45-59.

Lemov, Doug (2015). Teach Like A Champion 2.0. San Francisco, CA. Jossey-Bass, p 64.

Marzano, R. J. (2003). *What works in schools: Translating research into action*. Alexandria, VA: Association for Supervision and Curriculum Development.

Mehrabian, Albert; Wiener, Morton (1967). "Decoding of Inconsistent Communications." *Journal of Personality and Social Psychology*. 6 (1): 109-114.

Morgan, Marlon (2019). Trauma Informed Practices Presentation. Wellness Together. Rocklin, CA.

Muhammad, Anthony (2009). Transforming School Culture: How to Overcome Staff Division. Bloomington, IN. Solution Tree Press.

National Center for Mental Health Promotion and Youth Violence Prevention, "Childhood Trauma and Its Effect on Healthy Development," July 2012 (http://sshs.promoteprevent.org/sites/default/files/trauma_brief_in_final.pdf)

Nayaran, AJ, Rivera LM, Berstein, RE, Harris, WW, & Lieberman, AF. (2017). "Positive childhood experiences predict less psychopathology and stress in pregnant women with childhood adversity: A pilot study of the benevolent childhood experiences (BCEs) scale. Child Abuse and Neglect.

Olisa, B. & Ogunlade, A. (2018). Floating Schools, Nigeria. Impact Journalism Day. Retrieved from: http://impactjournalismday.com/story/floating-schools/

Piaget, Jean & Inhelder, Barbel (1958). The Growth of Logical Thinking From Childhood to Adolescence, translated by A Parsons and S. Seagrin. New York. Basic Books.

Puentedura, Ruben R. (2015). SAMR: A Brief Introduction. Eanes ISD Digital Learning. Retrieved from: http://hippasus.com/blog/archives/227

Reeve, J., Jang, H., Carrell, D., Jeon, S., & Barch, J. (2004). Enhancing students' engagement by increasing teachers' autonomy support. Motivation and Emotion, 28(2), 147-169.

Reeves, Douglas B. (2006). The Learning Leader: How to Focus School Improvement for Better Results. Alexandria, VA. ASCD

Rowley, R., & Wright, D.W. (2011). No "White" Child Left Behind: The Academic Achievement Gap between Black and White Students. Journal of Negro Education. Vol. 80 Issue 2, 93-107.

Shin, Aung (2013). Education gets a boost. Myanmar Times. Retrieved from: https://www.mmtimes.com/special-features/165-back-to-school-2013/6747-education-budget-boost-is-it-enough.html

Starratt, Robert (2004). Ethical Leadership. San Francisco, CA. Jossey-Bass.

Todorov, A. & Willis, J. (2006). "First Impressions: making up your mind after a 100-ms exposure to a face." Psychological Science. 17(7). 592-598.

Urbano, Lensyl (2011). Zipline to School. Montessori Muddle. Retrieved from: http://montessorimuddle.org/2011/09/03/zipline-to-school/

Wastlund, Erik (2007). Experimental studies of human-computer interaction: working memory and mental workload in complex cognition. Goteborg University. Retrieved from http://hdl.handle.net/2077/4693

Weller, Chris (2016). The 14 most innovative schools in the world. Business Insider. Retrieved from: https://www.businessinsider.com/most-innovative-schools-in-the-world-2-2016-10

Wong, H. & Wong, R., (1998). *How to be an effective teacher: The first days of school.* Mountain View, CA: Harry K. Wong Publications, Inc.